JOURNEYS INTO
MEDIEVAL ENGLAND

Whitby Abbey, Yorkshire.

OURNEYS INTO

EDIEVAL

NGLAND

Written and photographed by

MICHAEL JENNER

A MERMAID BOOK

Also by Michael Jenner

YEMEN REDISCOVERED
BAHRAIN - GULF HERITAGE IN TRANSITION
SYRIA IN VIEW
SCOTLAND THROUGH THE AGES
LONDON HERITAGE
A TRAVELLER'S COMPANION TO THE WEST COUNTRY
THE ARCHITECTURAL HERITAGE OF BRITAIN AND IRELAND

MICHAEL JOSEPH LTD

Published by the Penguin Group, 27 Wrights Lane, London W8 5TZ, England
Viking Penguin Inc., 375 Hudson Street, New York, New York 10014, USA
Penguin Books Australia Ltd, Ringwood, Victoria, Australia
Penguin Books Canada Ltd, 10 Alcorn Avenue, Toronto, Ontario, Canada M4V 3B2
Penguin Books (NZ) Ltd, 182-190 Wairau Road, Auckland 10, New Zealand

Penguin Books Ltd, Registered Offices: Harmondsworth, Middlesex, England

First published in Great Britain April 1991
First published in Mermaid Books 1994

Typeset in Linotron 11/13.25pt Concorde Roman by Goodfellow & Egan Ltd, Cambridge
Colour reproduction by Anglia Graphics, Bedford
Printed and bound by Kyodo Printing, Singapore

A CIP catalogue for this book is available from the British Library
ISBN 0 7181 3678 0

Page 1: Saxon Sculpture, Breedon-on-the-Hill, Leicestershire

To our medieval ancestors, without whom
this book would not have been possible.

Beverley Minster, Yorkshire.

A Cistercian masterpiece, Rievaulx Abbey in Yorkshire.

CONTENTS

The Chapter House, Southwell Minster, Nottinghamshire.

ACKNOWLEDGEMENTS

TRAVEL AND FIELD RESEARCH the length and breadth of England were greatly facilitated by the guidance and assistance of the British Tourist Authority and the Regional Tourist Boards of Cumbria, East Midlands, Northumbria, North West, South East, West Country and Yorkshire and Humberside; also of the Tourist Information Centres of Hexham and Norwich and the Tourism Officers of Alnwick, Berwick-upon-Tweed, Castle Barnard, Lincoln and Norwich. Thanks are also due to the custodians of the many parish churches and cathedrals visited and photographed in the course of the work on this book. Likewise the National Trust and English Heritage are acknowledged for their painstaking and enlightened conservation and presentation of so many of England's finest medieval monuments. Finally, the dedication of numerous private owners of castles and manor houses should be saluted for doing so much to keep at bay the inevitable ravages of time and to carry forward the physical message of the Middle Ages into the next millennium.

A KNIGHT RIDES OUT. *An exquisite miniature carving of an armoured nobleman on horseback adorns the tomb canopy of Aymer de Valence in Westminster Abbey.*

A VENERABLE HOAX. *The wooden seat in St Paul's, Jarrow, allegedly used by Bede, has been shown to date many centuries after the death of the saintly scholar.*

A TRIPLE LANCET. *The soaring purity of line of Gothic's Early English phase makes a dramatic appearance at Egglestone Abbey in County Durham.*

BUILT TO ENDURE. *The curtain wall and towers of Warwick Castle's fourteenth-century fortifications have survived remarkably intact.*

United for eternity. Tomb effigies at Spilsby, Lincolnshire.

INTRODUCTION

TO THE MODERN MIND the very concept of the Middle Ages implies a state of transition or a cultural and historical interspace between the demise of the Classical Age and its eventual rebirth or Renaissance. It need hardly be said that the people of the Middle Ages did not see themselves as a mere filling in a cultural sandwich. They both lived for the day and built for eternity, though the imminent end of their world was ever a matter of fear and foreboding. However, the label of the Middle Ages has stuck, albeit with divergencies of opinion as to the beginning and end of the period. Within the context of England we can extend the Middle Ages right back to Saxon times and the gradual extinction of Celtic culture, but for most of us 'medieval' starts in or around 1066 with the Norman Conquest and lasts for something in excess of four hundred years. For some scholars, the crucial terminal date for the waning of the Middle Ages is 1485 when Henry Tudor plucked the crown of England from a thorn bush at Bosworth Field and quashed the ambitions of the last of the Plantagenet monarchs, Richard III. But this was really just the beginning of the end, a lengthy process which was finally brought to its logical culmination fifty years later during the reign of Henry VIII. This book is not dogmatic about dates and allows the Middle Ages to embrace all that lies between the Dark Ages and the Renaissance; but the heart of the subject matter is contained between the eleventh and the fifteenth century.

Today's popular view of medieval England is decidedly romantic, as if by recoiling from the harsh realities of the present we hope to find a safe refuge in the past. Accordingly, the Middle Ages conjure up a scenario of battlemented castles with lofty towers, knights in armour, courtly tournaments, noblemen hunting stags, ladies stitching tapestries, Gothic cathedrals whose soaring vaults resound to the chanting of psalms and parish churches clinging limpet-like to the face of the land, defying the passage of time. The dream is also given substance by the ancient moated manor houses of the gentry, ivy-clad and secretive, with their great halls, minstrel galleries, carved screens, cavernous fireplaces and roofs of oak beams. Stone and brass effigies of generations of ancestors gaze up at us with world-weary expressions. Dotted about the countryside are the mutilated ruins of hundreds of abbeys and priories where Benedictines, Augustinians, Cistercians and Carthusians lived out their days in religious service dedicated to the glory of God. The whole period, remote and unattainable, has all the qualities of an illuminated manuscript of heartrending beauty.

But there is the reverse of the medal to be considered. For all the idealised glamour and chivalry there was the attendant squalor and cruelty. For the banqueting hall there was also the torture chamber. For every noble lord and lady in the castle there were countless unfortunate wretches at their gate. For every pious religious spirit there was a knave or a rogue waiting to prey on the innocent. And for every item of ethereal artistry there were the ugliest scenes of human suffering to be imagined. Youth was short and quickly spent. Death stalked the living at every step, not just in the course of bloody feuds and dynastic wars but also in the outbreaks of plagues and epidemics, of which the notorious Black Death was but the worst of many horrific visitations.

Generally speaking, the negative aspects of the Middle Ages have been erased from the landscape: the dead have long since rotted away whether buried or not. A deserted village is now more likely to inspire in us poetic reflections on the transience of human life than on the ghastly realities of the bubonic plague brought over by the fleas of the black rodent with the delightfully guileless name of 'Rattus rattus' which first came ashore at Melcombe in Dorset in the year 1348 and spread its deadly pestilence like wildfire to devastate and decimate the population, whether rich or poor, regardless of rank or station, age or sex.

Our main physical reminders of the Middle Ages are the great monuments of stone, the castles and cathedrals, churches and abbeys. That religious structures loom large in our present catalogue of medieval relics in England reflects the overwhelming pre-eminence of the Church not only as the spiritual authority in the land but also as a material power, a wealthy landowner, a shrewd property developer, patron of building and architectural pioneer. There was an element of jest in the contemporary saying that 'if the Abbess of Shaftesbury were to wed the Abbot of Glastonbury their heir would own more land than the King', for the matter was impossible to put to the test. But the essential point is beyond dispute: the monastic establishment acquired through centuries of donations, bequests and legacies a stranglehold on the economic apparatus of England.

The Dissolution of the Monasteries in the 1530s by Henry VIII was not a detail of ecclesiastical reform but a massive expropriation and redistribution of the property of the Church. It was this sudden transfer of huge estates all over the land from the monks and nuns to the upwardly mobile Tudor gentry which marked the real end of the Middle Ages. The subordination of the Church coincided with the absorption of Renaissance thought and culture to dispel the old superstitions and unscientific beliefs which characterised the preceding centuries.

The wholesale destruction of monastic property was not a gratuitous act of violence but a deliberate instrument of policy, 'for fear the birds should build therein again'. Some abbey churches such as Bristol and Gloucester survived as cathedrals; and many others such as Beverley, Cartmel, Selby and Sherborne continued in service as parish churches. But in the main, demolition was swift and efficient. The King's Commissioners claimed all items of monetary value such as silver and gold plate, jewelled ornaments and even lead from the roofs; but the exquisite woodwork, priceless manuscripts and carved statues ended up as so much fuel for the bonfire. No cultural annihilation by an alien power has been accomplished with quite the severity which English people meted out on their own heritage. Even good citizens joined in the clamour and the destruction. One participant at the despoliation of Roche Abbey, one of the fine Cistercian houses in Yorkshire, justified his actions with the argument: 'What should I do? Might I not as well as others have some profit of the spoil of the Abbey? For I did see all would away; and therefore I did as others did.'

Also victims of Henry VIII's offensive against the Church were the shrines of the saints: those of St Swithun at Winchester and St Thomas at Canterbury were not only robbed of their precious stones but were physically destroyed as well; their sacred relics were dumped without trace in some forgotten and unrecorded spot. With the destruction of these shrines one of the great institutions of medieval England, the pilgrimage, was brought to a brutal end. It is true that in the early sixteenth century pilgrims were far less in evidence than in earlier centuries, but during their heyday they represented a social and economic fact of the utmost importance. Such was the religious credit and prestige to be acquired from a pilgrimage that shrines the length and breadth of the land were avidly visited by hosts of supplicants drawn by tales of martyrdom and miracles. Donations at the more popular shrines amounted to amazing riches, sufficient to rebuild the cathedrals at Gloucester and Canterbury. Contrast the painful fundraising efforts of today to find the money to repair even a part of one of England's cathedrals, for example the endangered spire at Salisbury.

It was perhaps no coincidence that the first systematic exploration of England's past occurred in the 1530s, just as the death knell of medieval, monastic society was being sounded. At this time the intrepid itinerant scholar John Leland embarked on what his publisher called his 'laboryouse journey' or 'the serche of Johan Leylande for Englandes antiquitees'. Not that Leland was an archaeologist as such, but his interest in the past took him right back to the Celtic mists of the Dark Ages. He was a painstaking topographical recorder, and his travel notebooks, which he never managed to polish up into a coherent account – for he suffered a mental breakdown in his early forties – contain a wealth of detail concerning towns, villages, castles, manors, churches, cathedrals, monastic property, bridges, farms and landscapes. He listed the names of clerics, scholars, landowning gentry and feudal magnates; and some of the families in the last category still occupy the same houses as when visited by Leland 450 years ago.

Through Leland we gain our earliest comprehensive view of medieval England since Domesday: a patchwork of farms and estates dotted with towns and hamlets, a countryside still well wooded, although many of the great oak forests were then falling victim to the lumberman's axe to be used as beams and planks for ships as well as houses. But even if

RICH COLOURS STILL RESPLENDENT. *The heraldic devices on the Lovell tomb at Minster Lovell, Oxfordshire* (above), *are kept freshly painted. The stained glass at Fairford, Gloucestershire* (right), *has survived some five centuries.*

Gainsborough Old Hall, Lincs. – a lion in the oriel.

partly denuded of trees, England at the close of the Middle Ages was gloriously free of urban sprawl and ribbon development. Numerous are Leland's references to 'champayne ground' or open country. That sense of natural freedom and an uncluttered environment is perhaps the chief missing element which prevents us from reliving the reality of medieval England. Splendid buildings there are aplenty, but their context has been lost.

Nowhere is this more true than in the towns and cities where redevelopment and *Blitzkrieg* have taken a specially heavy toll. Even so, in towns such as York and Canterbury enough remains to suggest the rich diversity of medieval urban life, a cellular structure administered by the craft guilds and parish churches. This was a scene decked out with the symbolism of heraldry and carved figures in church and cathedral, decorated roof bosses, bench ends, lintels, spandrels, tomb chests and canopies. There were everywhere statues in niches, leering gargoyles, hand-painted signs, elaborate market crosses, ornate pargetting on façades, proverbs inscribed on exposed beams and door frames. Alas, where is the human language of today's cities to be read in the anonymous architecture? And where is the life and colour of urban existence in all those dead town centres given over almost entirely to banks, building societies and estate agents? Nevertheless, we must be grateful for the structures that do survive up and down the country, even if they are often only nostalgic shells without meaningful content.

Castles in remote country offer much more scope for indulging medieval fantasies. Bodiam in Sussex, Dunstanburgh in Northumberland and Restormel in Cornwall, among others, still stand aloof from modern life and give us the chance to imagine the castellar lifestyle, the noises and smells of stables and kitchens, the sweet notes of lute players and madrigal singers, the gorgeous wall tapestries and other furnishings which feudal barons and kings usually transported in a cumbersome wagon train from one castle to the next, consuming their rents in the form of produce and moving on when their household retinue had either exhausted the larder or overloaded the drains and latrines. As the Renaissance scholar Erasmus reminds us so powerfully, even noble late medieval houses in England were squalid affairs: the floors of their halls were 'strewed with rushes, beneath which lies an ancient collection of beer, grease, fragments, bones, spittle, excrement of dogs and cats, and everything that is nasty'. What we see today is, by contrast, eerily hygienic.

Although many medieval buildings, whether castles or abbeys, are now in a ruinous condition as a result of the wounds inflicted by the vagaries of history, we are still struck by the permanence of the architecture. It was an age which employed stone for all its major buildings and developed the art of masonry to unparalleled heights. Thus it is that the Middle Ages seem predestined to outlive the ensuing, flimsier productions of brick and stucco of Georgian and Victorian England. However, most folk of the middling sort lived in timber-framed houses that were simply assembled on site, and indeed could be moved on rollers like mobile homes. The father of the Tudor chronicler of London, John Stow, woke up one morning to find that his arrogant neighbour, the mighty Thomas Cromwell, mastermind of the Dissolution, had removed the Stow residence several yards in order to extend his garden.

The medieval masons' lodge rather than the carpenters' workshop was the élitist institution of the day and it stood in the vanguard of the technology that really progressed in the Middle Ages, that of building and architecture. The lodge was the workplace of those men who carried through the revolutionary transition from the round arch beloved of the Normans with its heavy, inert structures to the lighter, living and more daring pointed arch of the Gothic style. Thereafter, every possible variant of Gothic architecture was tried, from the austerity of Early English to the ornate intricacy of Decorated and the floating grace and elegance of the final Perpendicular phase.

But the technical ingenuity and sense of permanence should not delude us. Our ancestors were fallible humans working with simple tools, who arrived at new solutions by the old method of trial and error. Even the greatest of cathedrals arose almost organically over several generations as fresh styles and techniques were introduced along the way. Mistakes had to be either rebuilt or corrected by some additional work, as at Wells where the increased weight of the tower called for the insertion of those mighty scissor arches below. Nor was permanence actually achieved. Bits of buildings were always in need of repair, if not falling off. The noble spires of Old St Paul's and Malmesbury Abbey were struck down by storms. Lincoln Cathedral was entirely rebuilt after being split asunder by an earthquake; and even the mason-architects were not immune from danger. The first recorded industrial accident was that of William of Sens, pioneer of the Gothic style at Canterbury Cathedral, who fell from the scaffolding and died soon afterwards as a result of his injuries. It is the memory of such men and of the anonymous masons, who have left their marks and often their stone portraits in England's cathedrals, which makes a visit particularly moving an

ENGLAND'S MOST FAMOUS DESERTED VILLAGE. *The title must surely belong to Wharram Percy in Yorkshire which has been the subject of the most intensive archaeological activity in recent years.*

A BRIDGE TO THE PAST. *The fourteenth-century stone bridge at Stopham in Sussex is a lasting tribute to the skills of medieval engineers and architects.*

St Wystan's Crypt, Repton, Derbyshire.

experience. We sometimes talk of medieval folk as if they were a race of aliens, from a different time dimension, but their emotions and aspirations were recognisably ours, not at all removed from our own cares and preoccupations, as even a brief dip into Chaucer's *Canterbury Tales* clearly reveals.

To a certain extent this book is an exploration of a lost world, for there is no way of recreating a past age from the fragments we have inherited, plentiful though they be. But medieval England need be neither a dull history lesson nor a forlorn nostalgic indulgence. Great buildings and the spirit that raised them can still serve as a living inspiration; and we can appreciate the domestic details and decorative refinements of oriels, solars and great halls with the same delight that they imparted to the original occupants. Buildings that are both practical and beautiful do transcend time.

Fascination with the Middle Ages began almost as soon as the era itself receded into a memory. Perhaps Shakespeare was the first medievalist, for his historical dramas resound to the clash of swords wielded by medieval kings and magnates and his locations are castles and battlefields. There was a lapsing of interest in the seventeenth century, but by the eighteenth 'Gothick' relics had become a prized if eccentric curiosity in the landscaped parks of the gentry. In the nineteenth century the full-blooded Gothic Revival sought to revitalise Christian society by a return to the cultural values of the Middle Ages. The passion for things medieval continued unabated for the length of the century and has left us with a Victorian Gothic inheritance which is perhaps neither one thing nor properly the other.

In the twentieth century there has occurred a trend towards a cooler, scientific and archaeological analysis of the medieval period. Energies are now turned towards the investigation of household rubbish and cesspits to cast light on the diet and diseases of the Middle Ages. Mass burial pits from the Black Death, long forgotten Saxon waterfront palisades and the outlines of townhouses form the stuff of current activity. Documentary research is revealing that medieval towns were much more populous than previously assumed, veritable hives swarming with human activity. At the same time, the heritage industry has a keen following with its battle re-enactments, medieval banquets, and displays of jousting and falconry. The taste for the macabre finds many gruesome offerings in tableaux portraying medieval torture and suffering.

Yet the abiding theme of the Middle Ages is the Christian religion, growing apace from the narrow constraints of Saxon churches and those womb-like crypts at Hexham, Repton and Ripon to the mighty crescendo of Norman cathedrals such as Durham or the enigmatic symbolism of a small church like Kilpeck in Herefordshire. And so to the manifold marvels of Gothic. In the Middle Ages God was everywhere apparent, motivating both pilgrims and crusaders. Monks were in plentiful supply: 'A fly and a friar will fall in every dish,' went the popular expression. There can be no access to a real understanding of the Middle Ages without a recognition of the intensity of religious feeling which flowed into almost every act and every creation.

The main inspiration behind these *Journeys into Medieval England* has been the exquisite visual artistry of the legacy that remains to be discovered anew by each generation. So rich is our stock of art and architecture from the Middle Ages – despite the various attempts to destroy it – that a fat gazetteer would be required to contain all the sites and monuments. The idea of a series of regional journeys into the past came about as a natural way of providing a practical and exciting insight into what is so often presented as a dry subject of purely academic interest. It is by travelling in a physical sense that we can best absorb the spirit of the age, not as an abstract concept but as a personal experience through our own senses. Since it is the very essence of a real journey to choose one route in preference to another, so this account has selected places to illustrate different aspects of the Middle Ages. Each journey tells its own story, and as the narrative commentary moves from one place to the next, so items of interest in between have had to be omitted. What emerges is thus no dutiful inventory but a composite portrait in words and pictures of a resplendent chapter in English cultural history. Medieval England presents us with a vibrant tapestry, a beguiling vision of a remote age that demands our admiration and respect; and what this book proposes above all is a direct encounter with some of the many relics of that precious artistic achievement.

Graceful vaulting springs from a corbel in Southwark Cathedral.

I. LONDON

'LONDON, THOU ART the flower of cities all' was the unequivocal opinion of the Scottish poet William Dunbar in 1501. The late medieval capital of the prosperous realm of England had already outstripped most of its European rivals and was poised for further dynamic growth during the Tudor period. However, that very dynamism, together with natural and man-made disasters, has conspired to rebuild the city several times over in the course of the intervening centuries, so that it requires some effort to recapture the atmosphere and urban cohesion of medieval London from the surviving fragments. Indeed, first impressions might suggest that the Middle Ages in this constantly booming metropolis are quite literally dead and buried. For example, the current controversy over the historic skyline of the City focuses essentially on the London rebuilt after the Great Fire of 1666 which is now roughly 300 years old. We are so concerned by the developments affecting Wren's St Paul's that its Gothic predecessor is all but forgotten. Until its spire collapsed in 1561, its great height of 450 feet far exceeded that of the subsequent dome at 363 feet. William of Malmesbury, writing in the first half of the twelfth century, described Old St Paul's as 'worthy of being numbered amongst the most famous of buildings'. Moreover, it represented the very heart as well as the soul of medieval London to an extent not emulated by its successor. But despite such losses London still offers the medievalist a satisfying experience.

Let us approach from **Southwark** where the modest cathedral is now hemmed in between a railway viaduct and the vegetable market but was once the centre of a thriving autonomous faubourg where the writ of the City fathers did not run. This was a lively place, packed with raucous taverns and inns much frequented by pilgrims before setting off for Canterbury and the shrine of St Thomas Becket. Chaucer's group stayed at the Tabard, its site now marked by a plaque at Talbot Yard in Borough High Street; but nearby the George Inn still conveys some idea of a galleried courtyard hostelry of the period although the present buildings date only from 1676. Such inns were used by itinerant companies of actors to stage dramas; and Southwark, on account of its laxer regime, became the favoured resort of the theatrical profession in Tudor times with such renowned establishments as the Globe and the Rose whose rediscovered site is to be preserved.

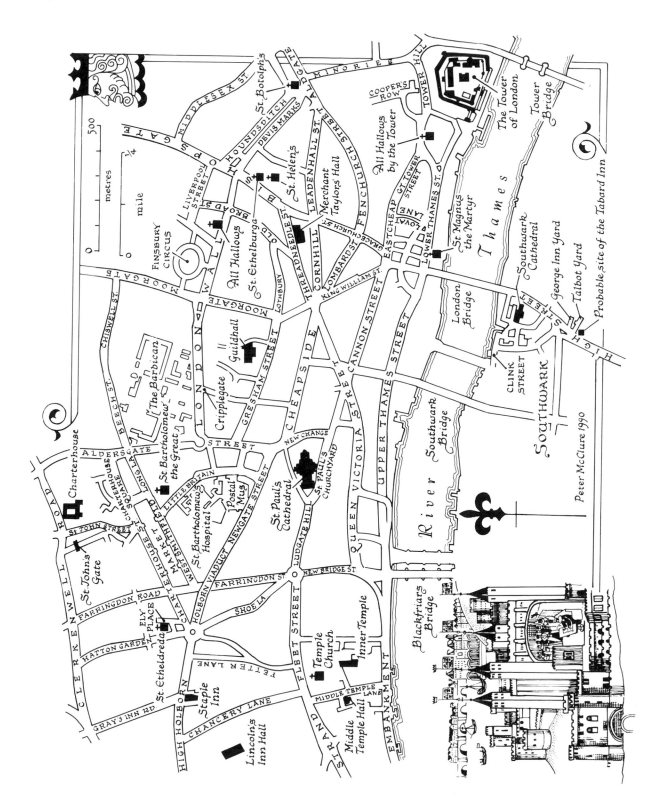

In Southwark actors and their riotous audiences disported themselves cheek by jowl with such mighty neighbours as the Bishop of Winchester. An evocative relic of **Winchester Palace**, a fine rose window of the Great Hall, has survived in Clink Street. But in this neighbourhood it is really **Southwark Cathedral** which must claim our attention. It has been extensively restored and rebuilt since its foundation as the Augustinian Abbey of St Mary Overie, but it retains its original retro-choir of Early English vaulting, still alive with the austere elegance and exuberance that sprang from the new building technology of the pointed arch. The cathedral contains other testimonials of rather different aspects of the medieval world. Some of the huge carved wooden bosses which once adorned the roof are now displayed at eye level to allow a close-up view of a veritable rogues' gallery of grotesque faces. These would once have leered down on the congregation from their lofty vantage point, a typically medieval accommodation of the ugly and the profane within a religious context.

Southwark Cathedral also provides a gripping illustration of another leitmotif of medieval art: the stark portrayal of death. In deliberate contrast to the idealised knightly effigies of the noble deceased, we are presented here with one of those sculptural renderings of the physical decomposition of the body as the flesh withers away and the bones press hard against the skin.

But it is better not to dwell too much on the macabre side of the picture. Our medieval ancestors knew that life was short, and it was lived to the full in a city such as London which offered all the pleasures of an earthly paradise along with the horrific visions of suffering and mortality. One of London's earliest chroniclers, William FitzStephen, writing in the 1170s, leaves us in no doubt as to the merits and charms of this burgeoning city on the Thames just one century after the Conquest:

> Amid the noble cities of the world, the City of London, throne of the English kingdom, is one which has spread its fame far and wide, its wealth and merchandise to great distances, raised its head on high. It is blessed by a wholesome climate, blessed too in Christ's religion, in the strength of its fortifications, in the nature of its site, the repute of its citizens, the honour of its matrons; happy in its sports, prolific in noble men.

Amid such fulsome praise FitzStephen* does give some valuable description of the London of his day such as the host of parish churches and monastic houses and the colourful scene of the various trades each occupying its own particular area.

A rather different scene awaits today at the northern end of the modern London Bridge which lies slightly upstream of its Roman and medieval ancestors. FitzStephen would have witnessed the construction of the famous stone bridge of nineteen arches commenced in 1176 which eventually became home to an entire community of more than 130 shops and houses up to seven storeys in height. In the middle stood a chapel dedicated to the martyred archbishop St Thomas Becket who was London's most popular saint throughout the Middle

---

*FitzStephen served as clerk to Thomas Becket, and like his master he was of Norman extraction but a native of London. 'I was a fellow-citizen with my Lord, one of his clerks, and an inmate in his family.' 'I was an ocular witness of his martyrdom at Canterbury.'

POWER POLITICS IN STONE. *The Norman architecture of the White Tower* (above), *though since prettified, still strikes its intended note of warning. The mighty choir of St Bartholomew-the-Great* (right) *received its elegant oriel window in the sixteenth century.*

Ages. During this time **London Bridge** provided the only fixed crossing over the Thames to the City, a situation which greatly benefited the navy of ferrymen, a tough and vocal body of men who opposed any scheme for a second bridge. The waterfront would have been buzzing with activity round the clock as much of the nation's trade passed over London's wooden wharves. FitzStephen gives us a fancifully penned inventory of the luxury imports: 'The Arab proffers gold, the Sabaean spice and incense; arms the Scythian. Thy rich soil, O Babylon, gives oil from the fertile palm trees, and the Nile precious stones; the Chinese send garments of purple silk, the French their wines; the Norse and Russians vair, gris and sable.' Now almost the only regular movement of cargo along the Thames is London's garbage which is removed by the bargeload on the high tide.

A short distance to the east of London Bridge, the seventeenth-century church of **St Magnus the Martyr** marks the emplacement of the old bridge; and in its churchyard some of the ancient stones have been preserved as precious souvenirs. The dedication to St Magnus recalls the Scandinavian intervention in London's affairs long before the Norman Conquest, but the present church is not at all medieval, being one of Wren's new buildings after the Great Fire. Henry Yvele, London's most prolific medieval architect, was buried here in 1400.

Proceeding eastward along Lower Thames Street, it is instructive to take a look at **Lovat Lane**, one of several curving alleyways which lead up to **East Cheap**, site of one of London's great markets along with **Cheapside**, further to the west. Although not one medieval house is still standing here, Lovat Lane manages to suggest something of the scale of the ancient townscape with its intimate grouping of varied frontages. Furthermore, this is the only street in the City where the rainwater still drains away through a central gulley. As we make our way slowly towards the Tower through a district now bereft of inhabitants, it is hard to believe that this was once one of the most populous corners of London with thousands of people crammed into a few streets. Here, by the wine warehouses, was one of FitzStephen's favourite haunts, 'a public cookshop' on the waterfront. But there is no point in looking for it today; and even the riverbank is no longer in the same place, since the wharves have made steady progress into the river over the centuries and left the original shoreline more than 100 yards inland.

The **Church of All Hallows by the Tower** contains a unique memento of pre-Conquest London in its one surviving Saxon arch which in its turn provides a link with Londinium, for it incorporates recycled Roman tiles. We are now within sight of the **Tower of London**. The original Norman keep, commenced in 1078 by William the Conqueror 'against the restlessness of the large and fierce populace', loomed large over London. Even the ebullient FitzStephen checks his bubbly tone for a moment while he describes it as 'a very great and most strong Palatine Tower, whose turrets and walls do rise from a deep foundation; the mortar thereof being tempered with the Blood of Beasts'. Now known as the White Tower, it forms the central stronghold within a rambling circuit of curtain wall and towers locked within a concentric ring of fortifications. The name of White Tower derives possibly from its bright stone from Caen in Normandy but principally from the practice begun by Henry III of white-washing the exterior, presumably in order to intensify the overwhelming effect.

Even now the Tower of London evokes images of confinement, torture and death, but the Norman keep was conceived as a fortified palace which offered most gracious and comfortable accommodation by the standards of the day. Its external aspect was slightly modified between 1663 and 1709 when Sir Christopher Wren enlarged the narrow Norman windows. The interior contains an authentic jewel of Norman architecture in the spartan vaults of **St John's Chapel.** John Stow, the Elizabethan historian whose *Survey of London* of 1598 contains the observations of a long lifetime, supplies a description of it: 'This ascends by a great many steps. It is darksome, and venerable for the Pillars, which are very Antique, and of the plainest Order, and the Capitals of them different. Now it is only used for repositing the old Records, where they lye in Dust and Confusion.' The round apse of St John's Chapel protrudes from the square structure of the White Tower in the south-east corner.

St John's Chapel, Tower of London.

The Tower of London occupied the eastern extremity of the medieval city and was the starting point for the city wall which encircled the entire settlement on the landward side. Against all the odds, substantial sections of the wall remain to be explored, although the medieval gates at Aldgate, Bishopsgate, Moorgate, Cripplegate and Newgate have all disappeared from the face of London if not from the map; but there is at **Tower Hill** the foundation of a thirteenth-century postern gate permanently exposed to view. From here a game of hide-and-seek with the old city wall can be played as we locate its scattered parts at **Cooper's Row**, where tradition has it that Alfred the Great repaired this bit of the Roman defences, then at **Bevis Marks** and in the churchyards of **St Botolph's**, **Bishopsgate**, **All**

THE GREAT TRANSITION. *The crypt chapel of St John's, Clerkenwell, encapsulates a turning point in architectural history. Framed by the round arches may be seen London's earliest example of a pointed arch.*

A ROYAL SIGNATURE. *The presence of the coat of arms of Edward the Confessor in the vaulted inner porch of the Guildhall suggests that it may commemorate royal patronage of an earlier foundation dating back to the reign of that monarch.*

Hallows and **St Alphege's, London Wall.** The modern road linking Aldgate, Bishopsgate and Moorgate follows the intramural circuit route created by Alfred the Great when the Saxons reoccupied the City in earnest. At Bishopsgate it is worth seeking out the tiny medieval church of **St Ethelburga** and the more generously proportioned **St Helen's**, both now totally dwarfed by highrise commercial buildings.

From St Alphege it is a short walk south to the **Guildhall**, still the municipal heart of the Corporation of the City of London. Sadly, the original fabric of London's medieval guild halls has been lost, but that of the **Merchant Taylors** in Threadneedle Street still sits on its original foundations and its notable crypt. The Guildhall itself – the father of the livery companies – conceals some fine medieval masonry behind its late eighteenth-century front, especially in the ribbed vaulting of the inner porch and the vast and magnificent crypt which dates back to the first half of the fifteenth century. The Great Hall owes much to the Victorians and the roof is actually post-war, but one of the original windows remains *in situ*, equipped with an inviting seat of stone. This is an excellent place to muse on the power and wealth of the City of London, whose citizens in FitzStephen's day styled themselves as 'barons'.

Returning to the city wall, there lurk within the forbidding concrete towerblocks of the Barbican some bastions of London's western defences, of which one sits prettily enough in an ornamental pool. This was doubtless the work of Henry III, for it is recorded that in 1257 he 'caused the wall of this Citie, which was sore decayed and destitute of towers, to be repaired in more seemly wise than before'. Another example may be inspected underground beneath the yard of the Post Office in Newgate Street. In this case the round medieval bastion of random rubble and mortar has been grafted on to a section of the Roman fort which guarded the approach to London from the north-west.

At this point we can abandon the wall and head north to London's most spectacular monument of the Norman period, the church of **St Bartholomew-the-Great** at Smithfield, a remnant of an Augustinian priory, one of the many religious foundations which clustered around the fringes of London like a monastic girdle and inhibited outward urban growth until the Dissolution. Most monastic properties in London were speedily gobbled up by the Tudor property men, but St Bartholomew's conspired somehow to pre-empt the confiscation of its entire estate by virtue of having previously made the hospital an independent concern. The present Barts, one of the great teaching hospitals in London, has its roots in the medieval hospice and infirmary founded 'to wait upon the sick with diligence and care in all gentleness'. One of its less fortunate patients was Wat Tyler, the leader of the Peasants' Revolt, in 1381. He was brought here after being stabbed by the Lord Mayor of London at nearby Smithfield. The King's men tracked him down and immediately prescribed a cure less gentle than that administered by the Augustinians, for he was dragged from his sanctuary and summarily beheaded. Even without the march of the rural peasants on London, the city was never short of rough and radical men; and neither King of England, nor Lord Mayor, nor even Bishop could afford to provoke the notorious London mob. The 'fierce populace' against which William the Conqueror built the White Tower remained a reality to be reckoned with throughout the Middle Ages.

As for the church of St Bartholomew's Priory, what we have today is essentially but the choir of a massive 300-foot long building. The nave was demolished at the Dissolution, but the eastern end was retained for parochial use. It ranks as one of the most compelling works of Norman architecture in the whole of England. The round-arched choir culminates in a rounded apse with an ambulatory which opens up some thrilling vistas. In 1515 Prior Bolton added his famous oriel window, from which he could presumably keep a watchful eye on the flow of donations at the tomb of the founder, Rahere. St Bartholomew-the-Great is still a thriving parish church, and it prides itself on its robust Norman architecture and on the fact that other City rectors come here to escape the ubiquitous Classicism of Sir Christopher Wren.

Just down the road is another monastic survival, the **London Charterhouse**, which has clung on despite remodelling as residence and direct hits by incendiary bombs in 1941. The distinctive layout of the Carthusian Order can still be traced in this ancient jumble of buildings. The doorway and serving hatch of one of the individual cells stand exposed in what was once the Great Cloister. Dating back to 1371, 'Cell B' – as it is called – is a tangible reminder that the Carthusians followed the rule of isolated living within the community. The survival of the London Charterhouse is due to its successive roles as school and latterly as a home for pensioners, known as the Brothers, whose daily round is supervised by the Master.

Clerkenwell, where the original Clerk's Well which gave the district its name can still be seen, has preserved some fascinating relics of the **Priory** founded in about 1140 by the Knights Hospitaller as their headquarters in England. The picturesque **St John's Gate**, a late reconstruction of 1504, gave access to the Priory of St John of Jerusalem. The purpose of this military Order was the defence of the Latin kingdoms in the Holy Land. The nave of their church in Clerkenwell was round, in imitation of the Church of the Holy Sepulchre in Jerusalem itself; its outline has been marked on the surface of St John's Square. During the Peasants' Revolt the Priory was burned and the hapless Prior carted off by Wat Tyler's men to Tower Hill where he was beheaded. The Priory was subsequently rebuilt, but the Order was eventually dissolved in 1540, causing the last incumbent to die of a heart attack brought on by the shock of receiving the news. The architectural interest at Clerkenwell resides in the crypt of the church which actually documents in stone the twelfth-century transition from the rounded arch of the Norman style to the pointed version of Gothic.

Returning to Smithfield, whose name comes from the 'smooth field' where a weekly horsefair was held, and down Charterhouse Street, we arrive at Ely Place where the intimate church of **St Etheldreda** takes us back to the year 1293 when it was built as a chapel for the Bishops of Ely who maintained a palace here until 1772. This was the Ely House of

LAWYERS FOR HIRE. *You can still engage the services of the legal profession at the same place as during the Middle Ages. The Old Hall of Lincoln's Inn dates back to 1490.*

TEMPLE OF THE KNIGHTS. *The Temple Church with its array of knightly effigies is one of London's most moving medieval interiors. The round shape of the nave is modelled on that of the Church of the Holy Sepulchre in Jerusalem.*

Shakespeare's *Richard II* in which John of Gaunt delivers his memorable lines:

> This precious stone set in the silver sea
> Which serves it in the office of a wall,
> Or as a moat defensive to a house,
> Against the envy of less happier lands;
> This blessed plot, this earth, this realm, this England.

In fact, John of Gaunt died at Ely Place in 1399.

Further west along High Holborn, at **Staple Inn**, a highly attractive albeit much restored group of half-timbered buildings shows the type of housing which proliferated in London just prior to the Great Fire of 1666. Thence to **Lincoln's Inn**, one of several Inns of Court established in the area by the legal profession, symbolically as well as practically located between the commercial muscle of the City to the east and the royal prerogative of the Court of Westminster. The Old Hall of Lincoln's Inn dates back as early as 1490. Slightly more recent is the **Middle Temple Hall** of 1562–70 with its double-hammerbeam roof.

Of overwhelming interest is the **Temple Church** of 1185, founded by the Knights Templar. Behind the round-arched west door of the church there is a remarkable circular nave, an exciting space which contains a curious blend of those newly fashionable pointed arches alongside interlaced variants of the earlier semicircular type. The Knights Templar, who wore the distinctive red cross on their white tunics, were immensely rich. Their principal purpose was to protect pilgrims to the Holy Land, but their vast financial resources gave them a commercial dimension as well. Many a wealthy nobleman not only endowed the Knights Templar most generously but also entrusted them with the safekeeping of his treasure. A basement chamber under the south aisle of the choir, itself a striking addition of 1240 in the Early English style, might well have served as their strongroom. The role of the Templars has been aptly likened to that of an embryonic Swiss bank of the Middle Ages, offering the maximum in security and secrecy. It is difficult, however, when contemplating the dignified, martial effigies of the Crusader Knights in the round nave of the Temple Church to detect anything remotely resembling our modern stereotype of the banker. The discipline of the Knights Templar was notoriously fierce: a Grand Preceptor of Ireland, Walter-le-Bacheler, was enclosed in a cell here and left to starve to death as a punishment for disobedience. The Templars were disbanded in the fourteenth century and their property passed to the Hospitallers who leased the Temple Church to the lawyers of the Middle Temple, to whom it belongs today.

The road to the west along Fleet Street and the Strand leads towards Westminster. Already in the late twelfth century the land between the City and Westminster had begun to fill up, for FitzStephen reports that the two were already joined together by 'a populous faubourg'. This area was particularly favoured by noblemen, bishops and other men of state for their 'lordly habitations'. As we take leave of the City, let us bear in mind that it was in the Middle Ages certainly a dangerous and unsanitary place as well as an exciting one. Recent research into population statistics suggests a population as high as 100,000 by around 1300, and all virtually packed into just over one square mile. FitzStephen's delight in the urban machine allowed him to note only two criticisms, 'the immoderate drinking of fools and the frequency of fires', but London must soon have grown into an overcrowded rabbit warren, perilous to pedestrians from pickpockets, muggers, muddy streets with unexpected potholes, stray dogs feeding on rotting carrion underfoot and with the constant danger of being doused by household sewage slung with only peremptory warning from the jettied houses overhead. Even horsemen were at risk, especially at night or in the fog, of being unsaddled by one of the countless low-hanging inn signs.

Westminster, on the other hand, was still a natural paradise according to FitzStephen:

Flying buttresses at Westminster Abbey.

Everywhere without their houses are the citizens' gardens, side by side yet spacious and splendid, and set about with trees. To the north lie arable fields, pasture land and lush level meadows, with brooks flowing amid them, which turn the wheels of watermills with a happy sound. Close by is the opening of a mighty forest, with well-timbered copses, lairs of wild beasts, stags and does, wild boars and bulls.

It was to this idyllic landscape that Edward the Confessor removed the Saxon royal palace from its previous location near Cripplegate; and it was here that he built his new Benedictine abbey between 1050 and 1065 on what was then a gravel island in the Thames, thereby giving the area its new designation as Westminster. Edward's Abbey of St Peter achieved great renown in its day since it placed itself firmly in the architectural avant-garde. As far as the Confessor was concerned, there was no need to await the Norman Conquest

SOARING GOTHIC. *The lofty nave and transepts of Westminster Abbey bear all the hallmarks of the pure Gothic style. Transparent and highly functional, the architecture is in a sense naked engineering.*

TUDOR ARTIFICE. *The new taste for daring intricacy is brilliantly exemplified by the Henry VII Chapel at Westminster Abbey, where a profusion of fan-vaulting bursts forth in a ceiling of complex stone patterns and in apparent defiance of the laws of gravity.*

before applying the latest in Norman building style and technology. **Westminster Abbey** was by all accounts a magnificent affair, but since it was systematically rebuilt from about 1245 we have to rely on contemporary illustrations for visual evidence. There is, however, one notable indicator of the abbey's original ancestor to be found in the dormitory undercroft called the Chapel of the Pyx or the Pyx Chamber and the adjoining museum. Here the characteristically squat, cylindrical Norman columns with plainish capitals and large square abaci support a heavy groined vault. Although but a subordinate element, it does convey the general appearance of the Norman style.

Contrast the ponderous solidity and repose of the Chamber of the Pyx with the lively grace and elegance of the octagonal Chapter House or with the soaring vault of the nave. In this juxtaposition we may comprehend the enormous leap forward that was contained in the transition from Norman to Gothic. John Stow thought this phenomenon worthy of mention in his description of Westminster Abbey, 'whose Arches turn not upon Semi-Circles, according to the Roman Manner of Architecture practised in our Days, but meet in acute Angles, in Imitation of the Gothic Way of Building'. Now this is a very early use of the word 'Gothic' to describe pointed architecture; and its implied meaning to a Renaissance man of the sixteenth century such as Stow was rather derogatory, for the Goths were clearly cast in the role of vandals and barbarians, the destroyers of Roman civilisation.

Our present view of Gothic and of Westminster Abbey is far removed from any hint of criticism: the great rebuilding begun by Henry III in 1245 and completed from about 1375 in the same style by the master architect Henry Yvele has bequeathed us one of our greatest national monuments. Thereafter the abbey underwent one more radical transformation when the Lady Chapel built by Henry III in 1220 was swept away to be replaced by another in the latest fashion of Perpendicular Gothic. The Henry VII Chapel, actually completed during the reign of Henry VIII, is a marvellous virtuoso performance of sixteenth-century fan vaulting. It was originally intended by Henry VII as a Lady Chapel, but it became much more of a royal mausoleum under Henry VIII and has accumulated a most splendid collection of tombs of kings and queens; but the shrine of Edward the Confessor remains the most prestigious, standing in its own chapel in the bosom of the abbey behind the high altar.

It was Edward the Confessor's removal of the Saxon palace to Westminster rather than the founding of the abbey which paved the way for London's future expansion to the west. Edward's new palace soon became the home of William the Conqueror in 1066. Its central feature was an aisled hall which was rebuilt at the end of the eleventh century by the Conqueror's son William Rufus. The new hall measured 240 feet by 67½ feet, being the exact dimensions of **Westminster Hall** today. Rufus complained that it was 'too big for a chamber and not big enough for a hall'. The roof was supported on a series of columns which subdivided the space into aisles. What we have before us today is essentially the same space, but although the lower parts of the walls belong to the building of William Rufus the hall as such was daringly reconstructed by Richard II.

The miraculous oak roof of Westminster Hall.

WEALTH OF THE MERCHANTS. *The signs of the material success achieved by some members of medieval London's trading community are still in evidence at Crosby Hall* (above). *Staple Inn* (right) *is an isolated reminder of the once typical streetscape.*

Gatehouse of Lambeth Palace.

In 1394 the architect Henry Yvele teamed up with the carpenter Hugh Herland to transform the aisled hall into a unified space spanned by a revolutionary hammerbeam roof of oak which required no support other than the heavily buttressed external walls. And so it still stands, vastly impressive in its spaciousness, empty of furniture or partitions, serving as a gigantic vestibule to the Houses of Parliament. Westminster Hall's only visual distraction, apart from the arresting sight of the hammerbeam roof itself, are the late fourteenth-century statues of the kings which peer down from their perches in the high windows.

Located symbolically over the river from Westminster stands the official London residence of the Archbishop of Canterbury at **Lambeth Palace**, which has become the administrative headquarters of the Church of England. Behind its 1490 gatehouse of Tudor brick, it reveals itself as predominantly Victorian rather than medieval, but it does contain a lovely crypt from the early thirteenth century. With the Thames to separate it from the Palace of Westminster, Lambeth Palace demonstrates the contradictory closeness and distance of the relations between Church and State.

It is stretching the medieval concept of London to continue any further west, and indeed to the purist London during the Middle Ages was only the City, but it is worth proceeding upriver to **Chelsea**, one of several villages along the Thames where the natural mode of transport would have been boat rather than horse or carriage. Here it is that we may discover the best preserved example of a medieval London merchant's home. **Crosby Hall**, dating back to 1466, originally stood in Bishopsgate where it contained both the family residence and business premises of Sir John Crosby. It was saved from the ignominy of demolition for redevelopment in 1908 when it was carefully dismantled and subsequently reassembled piece by piece at its new home by the Thames in Chelsea. Thus it escaped the threat of destruction during the Blitz. The 69-foot long hall which provided a most prestigious stage for commercial and diplomatic entertaining is now used as a hostel refectory by the British Federation of University Women. Apart from its truly spectacular roof painted in dazzling hues of red and gold, its other delightful feature is the oriel window, which rises the full height of the building.

But let us return for a moment to the London of the Middle Ages as represented by the City itself and imagine the endless spectacle of human life in that hugger-mugger of tiny neighbourhoods packed together in an urban honey-comb where the ramshackle houses of the poor leaned on the stone walls of noble mansions and monastic precincts. For this London was not yet segregated by class and income into separate districts, but enjoyed, for better and for worse, a rough communality. FitzStephen's so positive description of London would suggest that the 1170s were something of a Golden Age:

> I can think of no city with customs more admirable, in the visiting of churches, ordaining of festivals of God's honour and their celebration, in almsgiving, in receiving guests, in concluding betrothals, contracting marriages, celebrating weddings, laying on ornate feasts and joyful occasions, and also in caring for the dead and burying them.

But not everyone shared such a glowing opinion of London in the late twelfth century. The Winchester monk Richard of Devizes expressed a contrary view:

> I do not at all like that city. All sorts of men crowd together there from every country under the heavens. Each race brings its own vices and its own customs to the city. No one lives in it without falling into some sort of crime. Every quarter of it abounds in grave obscenities. The greater a rascal a man is, the better a man he is accounted . . . Whatever evil or malicious thing that can be found in any part of the world, you will find in that one city. Do not associate with the crowds of pimps; do not mingle with the throngs in the eating-houses; avoid dice and gambling, the theatre and the tavern. You will meet with more braggarts there than in all France; the number of parasites is infinite. Actors, jesters, smooth-skinned lads, flatterers, pretty boys, effeminates, pederasts, singing and dancing girls, quacks, belly-dancers, sorceresses, extortioners, night-wanderers, magicians, mimes, beggars, buffoons: all this tribe fill all the houses. Therefore, if you do not want to dwell with evil-doers, do not live in London.

A provincial view perhaps, but with all those temptations of London life to contend with, the attraction of a regular pilgrimage to Canterbury as a sort of spiritual antidote can readily be understood. So it's time to head back to Southwark and to follow the road taken by Chaucer's motley crew.

The Norman keep of Rochester Castle in Kent.

II. THE SOUTH-EAST

O THE MEDIEVAL MIND Canterbury meant one thing above all else: pilgrimage. After Jerusalem and Rome it was the most venerated of holy places; and among English pilgrims it was certainly the most visited as well. Chaucer's band of fourteenth-century pilgrims were thus embarked on the most popular of medieval journeys:

> . . . from every shire's ende
> Of Engleland to Caunterbery they wende,
> The holy blisful martir for to seke.

They were evidently not in a hurry to reach their destination; and indeed the *Canterbury Tales* end even before they reach the goal of their pilgrimage. In fact, for many pilgrims the journey was probably just as important as arriving. The verb 'to canter' derives from Canterbury, suggesting that it was an easy ride across the countryside rather than an arduous gallop. But to understand the Canterbury phenomenon and the overwhelming attraction of the shrine of Thomas Becket, archbishop, martyr and saint, it is necessary to bear in mind the intense belief in miracles, in the divine healing properties of holy relics and in the casting off of sin by physical contact with some saintly object.

Medieval England could be described as a society entirely composed of potential pilgrims in search of a shrine. Metal badges and other souvenirs were collected and sewn to a pilgrim's clothes rather like some people today put stickers on their caravans to show off where they have been. And there were some whose lives were spent in permanent pilgrimage, often undertaken by proxy for richer sponsors who stayed at home. The revenues from pilgrims to a particularly favoured shrine could be enormous, enough to provide the means for such massive rebuilding projects as the magnificent remodelling of Gloucester Cathedral in the Perpendicular style. Information about new shrines would quickly spread; and fortunes could be made if the public imagination responded. Winchester, Walsingham, Glastonbury and Gloucester all had their adherents at some stage but Canterbury was to outshine them all.

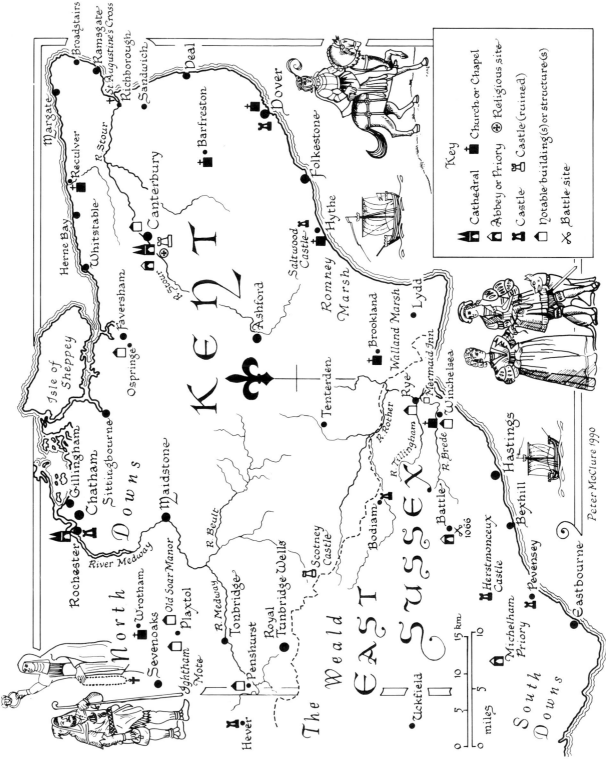

Key

† Cathedral   † Church or Chapel
🏛 Abbey or Priory   ⊕ Religious site
■ Castle   ⚏ Castle (ruined)
▢ Notable building(s) or structure(s)
✗ Battle site

Peter McClure 1990

Pilgrims flocked thither from all directions – even from the Continent – and the major routes were well trodden. Those from the west would have used the ancient track from Winchester across the North Downs and the Kentish Weald, known evocatively today as The Pilgrims' Way. For most people London marked the starting point for Canterbury, as it did for Chaucer's pilgrims. Nowadays, the Old Kent Road in south London and the A2 – albeit with some modern detours – still provide the essential route of one of the most potent of medieval journeys.

Rochester at the mouth of the Medway was, and remains, the principal attraction between London and Canterbury. **Rochester Cathedral** suffers by too close a proximity to Canterbury, but its noble Norman west front is compelling. Its shrine of St William of Perth once drew many pilgrims; the worn steps in the north choir aisle, polished and eroded by the knees of countless supplicants over the centuries, provide the only visible sign of the now vanished shrine's former importance. **Rochester Castle** dominates the cathedral at close quarters, almost too closely for comfort; but perhaps this enforced intimacy had something to do with the fact that both building projects were commenced in about 1087–8 by Gundulf, Bishop of Rochester, who had previously supervised the construction of the White Tower in London. But the great keep at Rochester, which is much more threatening in its uncompromisingly Norman four-square rectitude, was essentially the work of William de Corbeil, Archbishop of Canterbury, appointed in 1127 by Henry II to hold the castle. The custody of Rochester Castle remained with the Archbishop of Canterbury until 1215 when it was successfully besieged by King John. The south-east tower was undermined by sappers and later rebuilt by Henry III as a round structure less vulnerable to such tactics. From the outside the castle looks neat and efficient, but there is a brooding air of menace about the floorless interior of the keep where heavy Norman arcading and baronial fireplaces appear suspended in defiance of the law of gravity, as if by some dark and ancient spell.

After Rochester there is little to detain the traveller bound for Canterbury, but at **Ospringe** just outside Faversham there stands a fascinating sixteenth-century timber-framed structure containing parts of a hospital and shelter for pilgrims dating back to the thirteenth century.

By complete contrast to Rochester, at **Canterbury** it is the magnificent **cathedral** and not the castle which dominates the city. Its splendour must be seen as a direct result of the foul murder committed within its sacred precincts on 29 December 1170; for that was the event which sparked off almost four centuries of lucrative pilgrimage traffic. Henry II's epic quarrel with his former friend and protégé Thomas Becket, whom he raised to Archbishop of Canterbury, went far beyond personal animosity. The background to this clash of stubborn personalities was the conflict between Church and State. Becket, as the Archbishop of Canterbury, resolutely set himself against any reduction in the considerable secular privileges of the Church, which Henry was determined to subordinate to his own royal authority. After years of bitter wrangling the exasperated king uttered the fatal words: 'Will no one rid me of this low-born cleric?' The question was addressed to no one in

A MARTYR'S MEMORIAL. *Stained glass in Canterbury Cathedral commemorates the once famous shrine of St Thomas à Becket. This window shows in stylised form a group of pilgrims praying at the shrine.*

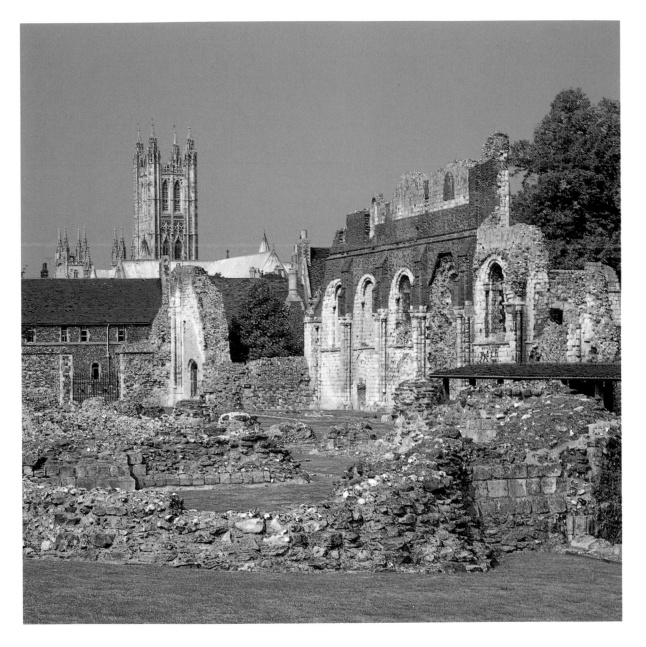

THE WHIMS OF FATE. *The ruins of St Augustine's Abbey in the foreground contrast to the magnificently intact fabric of Canterbury Cathedral. The former was a victim of the Dissolution; the latter, a beneficiary of a booming pilgrimage traffic over the centuries.*

particular but it was conveniently uttered in a way to be overheard by four knights who were loyal to the king and fierce enemies of Becket. Thus were the wheels set in motion and the stage prepared for the murder in the cathedral.

At Canterbury, Becket was informed of the approach of the four, Reginald Fitz Urse, William de Tracy, Hugh de Morville and Richard de Brito, who made no secret of their intent. They forced their way into the cathedral where Becket had decided to await his fate rather than take refuge in flight. At first, they tried to manhandle him out of the cathedral itself, for although their purpose was nothing less than murder, they were mindful of the principle of holy sanctuary which the cathedral conferred. Becket successfully resisted physical removal, not so much in a last-ditch attempt to save his life but conceivably in order to make his inevitable martyrdom as effective as possible, for such a bloody violation of God's house was bound to release shock waves of horror and outrage. Thus Becket faced his assassins, attended only by his chaplain Grim, whose arm was practically severed as he sought to ward off the first blow of the sword delivered by de Tracy. The fatal wound was the doing of Richard de Brito, who sliced off the top of Becket's skull. Then one of several figures in the background called Hugh Mauclerc stepped forward out of the shadowy gloom and disdainfully flicked Becket's brain with the point of his sword on to the stone floor of the cathedral. The spot in the north-west transept where the gruesome deed was performed is now marked by a commemorative stone.

Almost immediately came reports of miracles and cures accomplished by grace of Thomas of Canterbury; and thus was a militant archbishop transformed into a martyr and very soon a saint, his canonisation occurring on 21 February 1173. Public opinion in England and throughout Christendom was so horrified that Henry II found himself obliged not only to relinquish his attempts to subjugate the Church but eventually to do penance for the sacrilegious murder. Henry arrived in Canterbury in July 1174, some three and a half years after the event. Donning sackcloth at the church of St Dunstan outside the city walls and having removed his shoes, he proceeded barefoot for the last symbolic mile or so to the cathedral. It is reported that the king's tender feet were cut by the sharp cobbles and that he left a trail of blood where he walked as if in ritual atonement. Henry then permitted himself to be flogged by Becket's coffin, where he spent the night in prayer. At dawn he drank a cup of water containing a drop of the saint's blood, and he took away with him a phial of the same holy liquid when he departed. Not that Henry admitted to the murder of Becket: the extent of his guilt he acknowledged in a cleverly worded statement relayed on his behalf by the Bishop of London: 'He declares before God and before the martyr that he did not have Saint Thomas killed or murdered, nor did he command that he should be struck at or killed, but he freely admits that he did use such words as were the cause and origin of his being murdered.'

Just two months after Henry's theatrical act of penance the choir of Canterbury Cathedral was destroyed in a fire. This provided a timely opportunity to rebuild the east end of the church and to construct a worthy setting for the shrine of St Thomas which was removed from the crypt in 1220 and placed behind the high altar. The building work was financed by revenues from the booming pilgrimage traffic which placed Canterbury way ahead of its chief rival, the cathedral at Winchester, with its ancient shrine of St Swithun and the tomb of Alfred the Great, which had once been the most venerated in England. Money was lavished on the shrine itself: a garishly painted wooden outer case could be lifted by a system of pulleys to reveal a truly resplendent tomb adorned with gold, silver and precious stones. Openings in the structure allowed pilgrims to reach inside and touch the coffin of the saint.

All this vanished in 1538 when Henry VIII plundered every last item of material value, destroyed the shrine and secretly disposed of the relics of Becket, whom he denounced posthumously as a traitor. Thus was the battle between Church and State finally won by the latter. The space once occupied by Becket's shrine is now marked by a solitary candle and an inscribed stone. The floor around the vanished shrine is still covered with its decorative mosaic pavement of Italian workmanship, combined with roundels portraying the signs of the Zodiac and the labours of the months. This is what visitors would have seen ever since the opening decades of the thirteenth century; and the surface has been smoothed and buffed by the countless genuflections of pilgrims. Thus the real significance of Canterbury Cathedral may be said to reside in a physical void: the missing shrine of St Thomas.

In spite of Henry VIII's command that all images of the disloyal St Thomas be destroyed, some of the gorgeous stained glass at Canterbury Cathedral depicting scenes from his life and miracles has survived. Quite apart from the fascinating wealth of detail, the overall effect of deepest blue and red enlivened by flashes of yellow is a rich and satisfying spectacle of colour. So bound up with Thomas Becket is our present perception of Canterbury Cathedral that it is curious to reflect that the main part of the cathedral, with which Becket himself would still be entirely familiar, is the crypt from the early twelfth century, so extensive as to be almost a church beneath a church. It was here that the monks first concealed the Archbishop's body from his enemies and also where the original shrine was housed prior to the rebuilding. It was here that we may imagine the scene of an apparently contrite Henry II receiving the penitential lash. This is perhaps the most dramatic place in any English cathedral.

The rest of Canterbury's medieval heritage is overshadowed, physically as well as spiritually, by the cathedral. The castle was a modest affair by Norman standards; and its crumbling remains in the south-west of the city appear to be deliberately disregarded. Nonetheless, twenty-five houses were demolished of Saxon Canterbury to clear the 4½-acre site. Some stretches of the old city wall have been repaired, and the restored Westgate does convey the impression of an entrance to a genuine medieval city. In St Peter's Street the **Hospital of St Thomas the Martyr** is a precious example of the sort of charitable accommodation provided for poorer pilgrims. The Chequers of the Hope Inn, where Chaucer's pilgrims might have stayed when they finally arrived in Canterbury, is now partly

FOUR-SQUARE AND STRONG. *The imposing Norman towers of the church at Reculver on the north coast of Kent still provide a landmark for shipping.*

THE KEY TO ENGLAND. *This was how the strategic importance of Dover Castle in the Middle Ages was described. Its keep and bastions now provide an intriguing composition of light and shade, though the defences are now more symbol than substance.*

The remains of Greyfriars, Canterbury.

occupied by a jeweller's in Mercers' Lane. The loveliest relic of the period is the establishment of the **Greyfriars**, of which a sole surviving building straddles the River Stour. This formed part of England's very first Franciscan Friary, founded in 1224. Here, surrounded by peaceful gardens away from the bustle of modern life yet only a stone's throw from the centre of the city, it is easier than elsewhere in Canterbury to conjure up a picture of times past. The refectory of the **Blackfriars** is also intact and is now used as an arts centre by the King's School.

So great is the aura of Thomas Becket and Geoffrey Chaucer in Canterbury that the real founding father of the Church in that city, St Augustine, is easily overlooked. Yet without the missionary work of St Augustine there would have been no Archbishop of Canterbury and Becket might have found himself Archbishop of London instead; for it was to London that Pope Gregory despatched Augustine in the year 597. However, his reception at the court of King Ethelbert of the East Saxons at Cantwarabyrig was so encouraging that it was from there that he launched his famous conversion of the heathen English. Here it was that St Augustine refounded a church of late Roman date and sowed the acorn from which the mighty oak of Canterbury Cathedral was to grow centuries later. All trace of this building was finally obliterated in 1070 when Lanfranc, the first Norman Archbishop of Canterbury, inaugurated a total reconstruction.

In 598, very soon after his arrival in Canterbury, St Augustine also founded an abbey dedicated to St Peter and St Paul, whose subsequent ruins may still be seen just beyond the city wall to the east. The outline of Augustine's tiny abbey church is preserved amidst the ruins of several rebuildings which make this one of the most complex of archaeological sites to read. The significant point to grasp is that the Benedictine Abbey of St Peter and St Paul (known as **St Augustine's Abbey** since 978) was once more prestigious than the cathedral.

Until 792 the Archbishops of Canterbury were buried here, and the graves of the first five Primates of England have been identified, resting in the prestigious company of King Ethelbert, his Queen Bertha and Augustine himself.

St Augustine's Abbey was gradually upstaged by Canterbury Cathedral in the course of a long rivalry that often relapsed into acrimony, but it was the martyrdom of Becket in 1170 and the subsequent miracle-working at the shrine of St Thomas which was to leave St Augustine's Abbey forever in the shade. St Thomas, in the process of becoming the most popular saint in England, also ousted from favour Canterbury Cathedral's very own St Dunstan. As one looks across from the sparse ruins of St Augustine's Abbey, a victim of the Dissolution, to the splendid tower of Canterbury Cathedral, it is impossible to suppress the thought that Becket's martyrdom contained a blessing of sorts. The place and manner of his death made a heroic and lasting contribution to the future wealth and vitality of the cathedral.

Canterbury's early conversion to Christianity had much to do with its strategic proximity to the coast which offered the most convenient landfall for the crossing from Europe. At **Reculver** on the north coast of Kent, within the confines of a former Roman fort, there arose a Saxon minster around the year 669. Just a little survives of this church, which made liberal use of Roman tiles: it was remodelled extensively at the end of the twelfth century. To this period belong the impressive twin towers of the imposing west front which rise up dramatically from the very brink of the shore, for the sea has made considerable inroads into the defensive wall left by the Romans. Tradition has it that Reculver was also a seat of Ethelbert's royal court; and the fragments of a once magnificent cross discovered here have been associated with the patronage of this Saxon king. If so, Reculver would have been an important stepping stone on Augustine's historic journey.

It seems most probable that Augustine landed near another Roman fort, that at **Richborough**, where the remains of a chapel, although not demonstrably early Saxon, are generally held to mark the saint's first scene of activity on English soil. But the sea is now rather distant and the landscape is dominated by the cooling towers of a power station and a drab industrial complex. There is little here to recapture the mood of Christianity's return to England, and to make matters worse, a railway line has lopped off the south-west corner of the site. Do not be too excited by map references to St Augustine's Cross at Ebbsfleet on the Isle of Thanet, which claims to mark the site of Augustine's landing. This can only be described as a not very ancient monument of dubious value, being a Celtic-style Victorian cross erected in 1884. St Augustine's actual landfall must remain a matter of conjecture, but the heart of his life's work and his lasting memorial belong to Canterbury.

Let us now leave the world stage of Christianity and explore one of the many parish churches of Kent which have no connection with any great event. Some ten miles south-east of Canterbury, at **Barfreston**, there stands a modest parish church which is remarkable for having escaped the heavy hand of improvers and restorers over the centuries. Its exterior

SKULLS APLENTY. *The eery bone crypt of St Leonard's at Hythe in Kent contains the mortal remains of at least 4000 human beings. It is thought that the ossuary was once an attraction for pilgrims* en route *to Canterbury.*

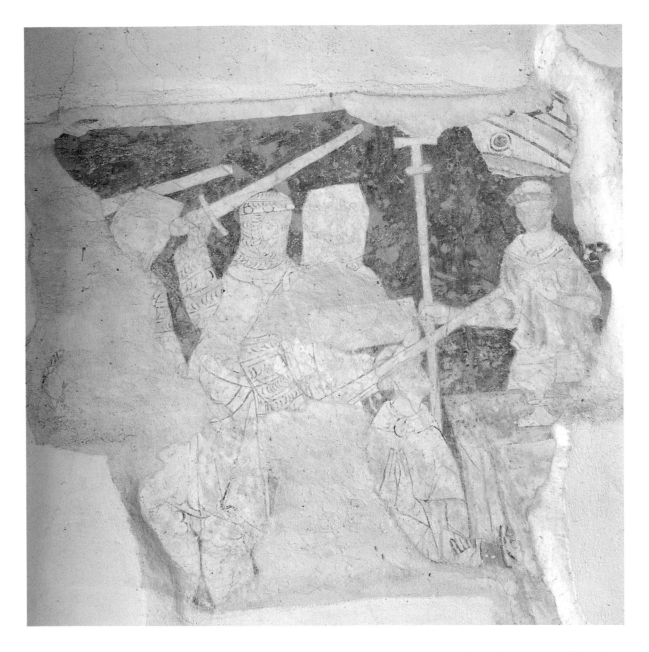

MURDER IN THE CATHEDRAL. *A recently uncovered mural in the church at Brookland in Kent shows Becket's moment of truth as the fatal blow slices through his defenceless skull. His chaplain looks on.*

belongs essentially to the last quarter of the twelfth century and presents a riotous assembly of sculpture comprising religious imagery, pagan mythology and everyday scenes of Norman manorial life. This marvellous three-dimensional picture book would have been a familiar sight to pilgrims who made the slight detour from the main road leading from Dover to Canterbury. Something of the wonderment it inspired may still be experienced by watching the morning light spread its rays gently across the south front, presided over by a tympanum of immense beauty. As the sun creeps slowly over the outer rings of the portal, so it coaxes into life the still-fresh carvings of Norman characters, such as a soldier with helmet and drawn sword, a cellarer filling a wineskin, a peasant digging the field, an archer with his bow and a musician playing the lute. At the top of the inner arch there is the figure of the recently canonised St Thomas of Canterbury. Then as the sun rises further and comes more firmly into the southern quadrant so it throws into relief the delicately incised features of the Christ in Majesty occupying the tympanum itself. First, the folds of Christ's robe are illuminated, then the Bible held in the left hand and then the right hand raised in blessing. Finally, the face emerges from the shadows and the full glory of the work is revealed, with its decoration of stiffleaf foliage and lively animals as rampant as in any hunting scene. Stepping back and looking up, you see the faces of a series of carved heads, mostly grotesque to ward off evil spirits. Some seventy come into view as you walk round the church, which appears to be contained by a neat string course like a wrapped parcel. It is no exaggeration to say that these carvings at Barfreston present a microcosm of the social and religious life of medieval England, which may still be easily and enjoyably read by any passerby of the modern age.

Time has stood still at Barfreston to an amazing degree, but not so at Dover, where the castle now watches over England's busiest cross-channel ferry port. A huge area is contained within the medieval ramparts of **Dover Castle** which sprawl majestically across the cliffs. The skyline is punctuated by the square keep of the 1180s built by Henry II and the equally square tower of the Saxon church St Mary-in-Castro, which abuts a Roman pharos which was partly rebuilt in the fifteenth century for continuing use as a lighthouse. Dover Castle's physical presence is so powerful that it still appears to afford symbolic protection to the south-eastern coast. The medieval chronicler Matthew Paris described it as 'the key to England'.

Further along the coast at the seaside town of **Hythe** awaits a unique glimpse into that macabre preoccupation with death that was ever present in the psyche of the Middle Ages. In the crypt of the parish church of **St Leonard**, perched halfway up the cliff behind the town are stacked some 2000 skulls and as many as 8000 thighbones. Assuming common ownership of the skulls and thighbones, it takes simple arithmetic to calculate that we are in the presence of at least 4000 deceased humans. While the exact provenance of the bones is unclear, it is accepted that they were all placed here roughly between 1230 and 1500. The collection may well have started as an attraction for pilgrims embarking and disembarking at Hythe on their way to and from Canterbury. A small donation from a steady flow of

The glorious south door at Barfreston in Kent.

MONASTIC STRONGHOLD. *The moat and gatehouse at Michelham Priory in Sussex afforded the Austin canons some degree of protection from the turbulence and insecurity of the times.*

GOD ON OUR SIDE. *This was the simple conclusion that William the Conqueror drew from his victory at Hastings in 1066. He founded Battle Abbey on the site of the conflict as an act of thanksgiving. The remains are noted for their superb vaults and undercrofts.*

visitors would have done much to boost the revenues of the church, and this is still the case today. The atmosphere of this ancient ossuary is not as depressing as might be imagined. Most of the skulls are arranged on shelves like jam jars in an old-style village shop; and one or two have been placed for obvious dramatic impact, grimacing out of the piles of thigh bones. One cranium even played host in recent memory to a robin's nest, showing that the dead can occasionally make a material contribution to the living.

Saltwood Castle, just two miles north-west of Hythe, made a brief appearance in the tale of Becket's martyrdom. It was here that the four knights met after arriving from France by separate routes, and worked out the details of their crime. From Saltwood they proceeded directly to Canterbury; and the rest is history. By one of those bizarre twists of fortune, Saltwood Castle was at the time still the legal possession of Thomas Becket by virtue of his office as Archbishop of Canterbury, but it had been seized by his most implacable enemies, the ruthless de Broc family. Thus it came about that Becket's murder was actually plotted in a castle belonging to the victim himself.

The ubiquitous Becket surfaces again, this time from beneath a coat of whitewash, at the village of **Brookland,** where in the parish church of St Augustine the exciting discovery was made in 1964 of a medieval wall-painting, portraying in graphic detail the assassination of the Archbishop. In the surviving fragment we can see quite clearly three of the four knights. The fatal blow to Becket's skull has just been struck. The victim is shown kneeling in an act of devotion with his chaplain Grim standing by his side and holding the archiepiscopal cross, emphasising for all to see the pacific posture and defenceless position of Becket, facts which were undoubtedly intended to magnify the horror of the sacrilege in the eye of the beholder. This is a precious example of medieval religious art combining didactic purpose and a dramatic picture of action.

The cobbled antiquity of **Rye**, a tight labyrinth of half-timbered quaintness clustered around the parish church, could not be bettered by the most inspired efforts of the heritage industry. The town regards both its charm and its antiquity as self-evident. The **Mermaid Inn**, in a gesture of apparent self-effacement, confesses through a prominent inscription that it was actually rebuilt as recently as 1420. The **Landgate**, built in 1329 by Edward III, and the **Ypres Tower** of about 1250 were both intended to play a part in the town's defences against the French. Rye was one of the Cinque Ports which provided ships and men for the defence of the south coast, but its own walls and ramparts were less than perfect, for the town was frequently attacked by the French, who in 1377 burned most of the town and made off with the church bells as booty. The sea has now withdrawn from Rye, and with it the danger of naval attack has also receded, but the place still conveys an impression of watchfulness from its lofty summit at the confluence of three rivers.

Neighbouring **Winchelsea** offers a contrasting version of medieval urbanism. It was conceived as a new town by Edward I after the harbour settlement of 'Old' Winchelsea, one of the original Cinque Ports, was destroyed by a violent storm in 1287. The new town was conceived on the grand scale and on higher ground; it was laid out in thirty-nine roughly rectangular blocks intersected by streets at right angles. Sadly, the silting of the River Brede put paid to the town's commercial prospects almost immediately and the economic potential of the venture was never realised. As a result, only a dozen of the blocks were developed at the time, and land was never at a premium. There is to this day a spaciousness and order to Winchelsea which create a most unmedieval effect. Indeed, the houses are post-medieval, although some thirty rest on cellars and undercrofts built in the thirteenth and fourteenth centuries to store wine casks. The most striking visual evidence of Winchelsea's failed ambitions is provided by the **Church of St Thomas of Canterbury**.

What we have left to admire of this building is magnificent enough, a splendid piece of Decorated Gothic architecture, but this is only the chancel of what would have been a veritable cathedral of a parish church, for the nave and transepts were never built. To add to its interest, it contains some of the most ornate knightly tombs, notably that of Gervase Alard, Admiral of the Western Fleet under Edward I, who died in 1310. The recumbent effigy in stone, most exquisitely carved and wearing a complete set of period armour, rests his feet on a miniature lion and holds up between raised hands a heart, a touching symbolic offering of his soul to God. The canopy above the tomb springs from corbels carrying portrait heads of Edward I on the left, and his second wife Margaret of France on the right, whom he married in 1298. This does not mean that Edward's grief for his first wife Eleanor, who died in 1290, was over. This was a political marriage between England and France; Margaret was young enough to be Edward's daughter and she openly sided with his children against him. But there they hover, disembodied heads carved in stone, as the guardian angels of Gervase Alard, and seeming for all the world to represent the ideal of conjugal union.

Nowhere along the south coast of England can the threat and the fact of invasion from France be ignored. Especially not at **Battle Abbey** which was founded by William the Conqueror in thanks for his victory over the Saxons at the Battle of Hastings in 1066. The abbey straddles the battlefield itself, and the exact spot where Harold fell mortally wounded with the arrow in his eye was commemorated by the siting of the high altar upon it by the express wish of the Conqueror. The abbey church later fell victim to the Dissolution; and part of the monastic buildings is now occupied by a girls' school. The most prominent surviving feature of the remains of Battle Abbey is the great gatehouse dominating the triangular marketplace of the town which grew up alongside it. The architectural highlights of the ruins include the novices' room at the south end of the dorter range and the monks' common room at the north end. These are brilliant examples of Gothic engineering virtuosity, a total delight for amateurs of elegant vaulting.

Further west along the coast, at **Pevensey**, stands the Roman fort which served William the Conqueror as a ready-made base camp after his unopposed landing on English soil. Thus were the works of those earlier invaders, the Romans, put to effective use centuries

MOATED MAGNIFICENCE. *Bodiam Castle in Sussex is undoubtedly the most picturesque of England's medieval castles. Less serious than it looks, it was built as the retirement home of an Agincourt veteran.*

AN ENGLISHMAN'S HOME. *Typical of England's many fortified manors is the delightful residence of Ightham Mote in Kent. The once defensive moat sets off the house to perfection.*

later by the invading Normans. A medieval castle was subsequently fitted into the south-west corner of the fort where William had quartered his troops. Defensive preoccupations guided the designs of monastic builders as well in this part of the country. **Michelham Priory**'s fourteenth-century gatehouse guards a bridge over a moat, behind which the community of Austin canons could enjoy some measure of security. Now that the danger of military assault has passed, the moat still confers the double benefits of privacy and picturesque effect. This is why the arrangement has been retained at a whole string of castles and manors throughout England; and the device is particularly well represented in the south-east.

Indeed, the title of 'moated magnificence' could be conferred both on the castle of **Herstmonceux** and even more so on **Bodiam**. The former is a brick-built pastiche of a castle but the masonry of the latter is the real thing and corresponds to everyone's dream image of the perfect medieval castle with its romantic battlements and towers of stone. Bodiam appears to float in a lake rather than be confined by a moat, so generous is the expanse of water which surrounds it. A total of three drawbridges have to be crossed before any besieger could tackle the barbican itself. But architectural historians tend to play down the martial functions of Bodiam and to stress the degree of domestic comfort installed by its builder Sir Edward Dalyngrigge, a veteran of the French Wars.

From the outside, Bodiam Castle presents itself essentially as it stood on completion in 1388. The marvellous authenticity is due to the fact that it was not converted into a post-medieval residence of any kind. It was slighted during the Civil War of the seventeenth century and thereafter mouldered away in ivy-clad oblivion until it was purchased in 1916 by Lord Curzon who repaired the ruins before bequeathing them to the National Trust. In a flight of fancy Lord Curzon penned what must be a common vision:

> At Bodiam . . . no trace of the modern world appears to invade the ancient and solitary beauty of the scene, and it could hardly surprise anyone, were a train of richly clad knights, falcons on their wrists and their ladies mounted on gaily caparisoned palfreys, suddenly to emerge from the Barbican Gate, for the enjoyment of the chase, or even were the flash of spearheads and the clatter of iron-shod hooves to indicate the exit of a party with more serious intent.

A flash of the same dream, albeit on a lesser scale, may be enjoyed at **Scotney Castle**, but here the remains have been reduced to a supporting role as a curiosity in an ornamental lake. **Penshurst Place** provides a perfect illustration of a medieval great hall of the thirteenth century with a central hearth; and its lofty oak roof is still in excellent condition. **Hever Castle**, lavishly over-restored by William Waldorf Astor at the very beginning of this century, might make the serious medievalist blush, but the general effect of this moated and fortified complex is most endearing.

Medieval authenticity in abundance may be experienced at the modest **Old Soar Manor** near Plaxtol. Here we can enter the vaulted undercroft, a solar and chapel belonging to a late thirteenth-century knight's residence tucked away in a fold of the Kentish countryside. The hall of this early medieval residential complex has been engulfed by the adjoining red-brick Georgian farmhouse. The solar – or private apartment of the knight and his family – is presented bare of any furnishing, thereby allowing a full appreciation of its spaciousness. The very fact of the solar means that the Culpepers who occupied Old Soar Manor from 1290 for some three centuries were quite well-to-do by the standards of the day. The windowseat of Bethersden marble at the southern end of the hall was a precious refinement.

The solar at Old Soar Manor near Plaxtol in Kent.

At Old Soar one can imagine something of the remoteness and isolation of rural life during the Middle Ages. The nearest village was four miles away at Wrotham where the Culpepers were buried in the parish church. At home the knight and his family were virtually cut off from the outside world but for news relayed by passing travellers. Here, a call to arms would have arrived like a bolt from the blue to disrupt the peaceful rhythm of daily life. Yet it was from places such as this all over England that knights were summoned to offer military service in times of war. The Culpepers owed rent and allegiance to the Archbishop of Canterbury who held the manor of Wrotham from the Crown in return for the obligation to provide three knights when required.

Nearby, at **Ightham Mote** the moated manor house has changed in external appearance very little since it was first built around the middle of the fourteenth century. After an active life of more than 600 years the house exudes antique charm, but sadly the ravages of time have caught up with it and a huge repair bill for essential work is the price to be paid for its survival. We are only a few miles from the London Orbital Motorway the M25, but at Ightham Mote and Old Soar Manor the modern world seems light years away.

Medieval streetscene at Lavenham in Suffolk.

III. EAST ANGLIA

T IS SOMETIMES SAID of East Anglia that it owes its pastoral charm to the fact that it is on the way to nowhere and is somehow mysteriously shielded from the modern world. This is at best only partially true today, but in the past it was quite the opposite. The flat coastline, riddled with rivers, was an open invitation to neighbours across the water in northern Europe both for commerce and for conquest. Conquest came first as Angles, Saxons and Jutes flooded over to challenge the ebbing power of the Romans. An image of the Anglo-Saxons as submissive serfs has adhered ever since their subjugation by the Normans, but the early settlers in Britain were fierce warriors, as adept with the sword as with the ploughshare. Witness the discovery of the truly magnificent boat burial of a Saxon chieftain with his armour and weapons which was discovered in 1939 at Sutton Hoo near Woodbridge in Suffolk. The body was probably that of the early seventh-century East Anglian King Raedwald who had converted to Christianity but later relapsed into paganism. There is nothing more than a bump in the ground to be seen at Sutton Hoo, but the exquisite jewellery and other artefacts among the grave goods are on permanent display at the British Museum in London.

Our next glimpse of the Anglo-Saxons conforms more to the popular image of those peasant farmers who laid the foundations of village society in England prior to the Norman Conquest. An aura of Saxon rusticity hangs over the church of **St Andrew** at **Greensted** in Essex. The nave of the church dates back to about the year 1010; it is a unique structure built of split logs of oak. Timber was once the most common material for churches in most parts of England, so this sole surviving example of the type has acquired a special value.

By contrast, there is at **Bradwell-on-Sea** a much earlier Saxon chapel built of stone and mortar. It stands within the confines of Othona, one of those coastal forts whose main function in the fourth century was to protect the shores of Roman Britannia from Saxon pirates and raiders. The chapel, which is dedicated to St Peter, is a simple barn-like structure; it was founded in around 654 by St Cedd, a Saxon monk trained as a missionary at the Celtic school of Lindisfarne in Northumbria, who was sent to preach the Gospel in the kingdom of the East Saxons. St Cedd's evangelising took him the length and breadth of eastern England, and he died eventually of the plague at Lastingham in Yorkshire. His tiny

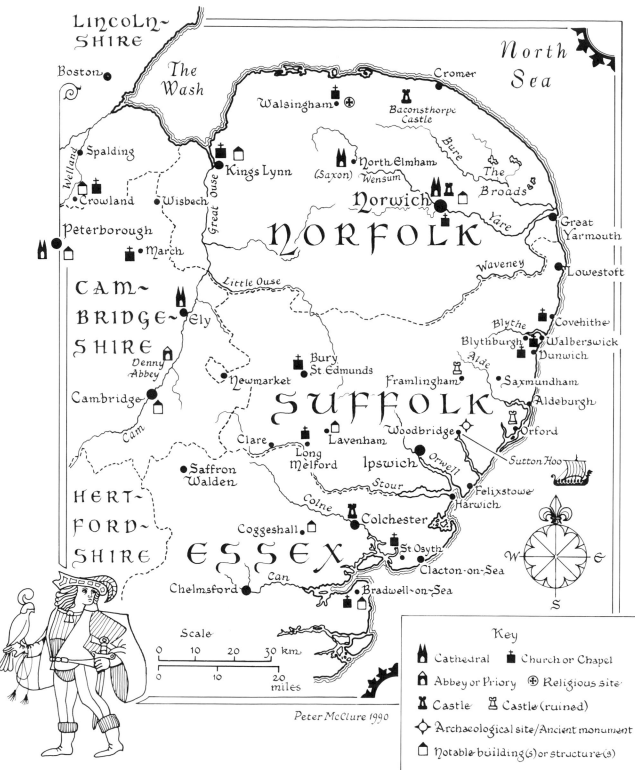

LINCOLN-
SHIRE

*North
Sea*

*The
Wash*

Boston

Walsingham

Cromer

Baconsthorpe
Castle

Bure

Spalding

Kings Lynn

North Elmham
(Saxon)

Wensum

*The
Broads*

Crowland

Wisbech

Norwich

NORFOLK

Yare

Peterborough

March

Great Ouse

Great
Yarmouth

Waveney

Lowestoft

Little Ouse

CAM-
BRIDGE-
SHIRE

Ely

Blythe

Covehithe

Blythburgh

Walberswick

Dunwich

Denny
Abbey

Bury
St Edmunds

Alde

Framlingham

Saxmundham

Cambridge

Newmarket

SUFFOLK

Aldeburgh

Orford

Cam

Clare

Lavenham

Woodbridge

Sutton Hoo

Long
Melford

Ipswich

Orwell

Saffron
Walden

Stour

Felixstowe

Harwich

HERT-
FORD-
SHIRE

Colne

Coggeshall

Colchester

ESSEX

St Osyth

Clacton-on-Sea

Can

Chelmsford

Bradwell-on-Sea

W   E

S

Scale

0   10   20   30 km

0   10   20
miles

Peter McClure 1990

Key

Cathedral   Church or Chapel

Abbey or Priory   ⊕ Religious site

Castle   Castle (ruined)

◆ Archaeological site/Ancient monument

Notable building(s) or structure(s)

St Peter's Chapel at Bradwell-on-Sea was rescued from oblivion and use as a barn in 1920 and is now the focus of an annual pilgrimage. Only the nave survives, but the outline of the round apse and of the side chambers, known as '*porticus*', may still be seen. This is a remote and lonely spot, only accessible on foot, and most conducive to evoking the mood of that most distant chapter in the story of Christianity in England. This is also a very rare memorial to the short-lived Anglo-Celtic communion before the Synod of Whitby of 664 ruled decisively against the Celtic and in favour of the Roman customs for regulating the Church.

The most lucrative source of wealth in medieval England came from the fleeces of the great flocks of sheep which grazed the lush pastures all over the country, but especially in East Anglia. Here the export of raw wool was soon followed by all the diverse activities of the cloth trade. One of many production centres grew up at **Coggeshall** in Essex, to which the arrival of the Paycocke family from Clare in Suffolk made a major contribution. The house built by John Paycocke at the beginning of the sixteenth century for his son Thomas on the occasion of his marriage to Margaret Horrold remains the most potent manifestation of the wealth and taste of these embryonic industrialists in places which are now considered as no more than rural backwaters. The elaborate carving both inside and out at Paycocke's is a swansong of medieval carpentry, soon to be rendered obsolete by the new fashion for brick, as may be witnessed by **Layer Marney Tower**, a grandiloquent Tudor mansion with a fantasy gatehouse of the most intricate brickwork built in 1520, to the general astonishment of the neighbourhood.

Colchester is no classic example of a medieval town, but its castle is a remarkable specimen of the hall-keep type. It was built in the 1080s for William the Conqueror, partly as a protection from Norse invasion, against which the Norse ancestry of the Normans provided no guarantee. Its construction was supervised by that most active of builder bishops, Gundulf of Rochester. Like the White Tower, **Colchester Castle** also contains a chapel with a projecting round apse, but its original facing of stone has been plundered, revealing the rough but solid core of flint and recycled Roman brick; for William's fortress was built on the site of the Temple of Claudius and it consumed vast quantities of its Roman predecessor.

The way ahead leads directly to more castles, but it is worth making a detour to **St Osyth Priory** near Clacton-on-Sea. The great gatehouse of this monastic establishment was rebuilt around 1475 with some excellent flint flushwork and a lively stone carving of St George in one panel over the arch preparing to despatch the dragon portrayed in a cowering position in another panel. Such opulent construction belonged to the closing chapters of monasticism in England as the years leading up to the Dissolution of the 1530s ticked away inexorably.

Returning to castles, the proud remains at Orford and Framlingham in Suffolk afford precious insights into castellar lifestyle of the twelfth century. **Orford Castle** rises high above the coastal marshes and provides a superb look-out to obtain early warning of the

ST GEORGE AND THE DRAGON. *This most popular of saintly legends is portrayed on either side of the gatehouse arch of St Osyth Priory in Essex. Note the attractive use of knapped flint combined with dressed stone.*

CASTELLAR COMFORT. *Living accommodation behind the curtain wall of Framlingham Castle in Suffolk was once provided in a range of separate buildings which have not survived the ravages of time as impressively as the outer defences.*

Norman urinal at Orford Castle, Suffolk.

approach of enemy shipping. It was built by Henry II between 1165 and 1172 against a threat of invasion, but also with an eye to putting Hugh Bigod, Earl of Norfolk, firmly in his place. The Earl had been obliged in 1157 to surrender nearby Framlingham Castle to the Crown. At Orford only the keep survives of what was an extensive complex, but this building is of tremendous quality, truly fit for a king by the standards of the day; and indeed it was the most important of Henry II's new castles.

The keep consists essentially of two spacious circular chambers, one above the other, which occupy the heart of the building, yet the real fascination of the castle lurks in the maze of passages, spiral stairs and tiny chambers which have been gouged out of the thickness of the walls. Orford also offers a fine opportunity to admire the sophisticated sanitary engineering of the period. The plumbing, being of stone, is still in excellent condition, built with an eye to stylish design as well as practical function. Latrines, drains and urinals have all been carved by skilled masons from solid stone; and even the outfalls at the foot of the keep have been discreetly embellished with round arches. The salty water from the castle well was supplemented by a supply of fresh rainwater collected from the roof and channelled into a cistern. This cunning arrangement had the added advantage of obviating the need for carrying water upstairs, since distribution could be organised downwards from the top. Alas, the military strength of Orford Castle did not live up to its domestic refinements: it was captured and held for a while by the French in 1217 during the fighting that followed the death of King John.

Framlingham Castle, further inland, provides a textbook illustration of the curtain wall version of defence. The internal buildings, none of which survive in their original form, would have abutted against the outer wall. This, with its thirteen towers, formed a circular fighting platform. Numerous arrowloops allowed the defenders to fire at the most oblique of angles. In times of peace the knights of Framlingham could ride out directly into the adjacent deer park for hunting; the stone supports of the bridge across the now empty moat stick up like prehistoric megaliths. Framlingham Castle became the focus of national politics in the summer of 1553 when Mary Tudor stayed here, waiting on the call to ascend the throne of England.

We now approach what is today an obscure stretch of the Suffolk coastline, but which in the later Middle Ages was an animated commercial scene with the export of cloth from a variety of estuarine ports to Europe and an equally valuable import of luxury goods in return to satisfy the demanding taste of the wealthy clothiers. The lazy Suffolk rivers provided safe and convenient highways to the cloth centres of the hinterland, but nature was all too often capricious and unpredictable. The prosperity of **Dunwich** was cut short in the fourteenth century when the River Blyth opted to take a different course to the sea, leaving the harbour silted up, and its ships high and dry. The cloth trade transferred mainly to Walberswick, Blythburgh and Covehithe which all boomed in the fifteenth century; but when business eventually declined these places sank back into a relative obscurity.

The only indication today of their erstwhile pre-eminence lies in the huge churches which dwarf their tiny villages. **Holy Trinity, Blythburgh** is like an ocean liner berthed in a fishing cove. This is a majestic fifteenth-century church in the Perpendicular style, full of light flooding in through its vast clerestory to illuminate a timber roof alive with angels. The death knell of Blythburgh as an active port was sounded by the introduction of bigger ships with deeper draughts which could not navigate the shallow channel to the port. By the sixteenth century the huge church was already something of a white elephant; and it suffered in the seventeenth century from the vandalism of Cromwell's soldiers who used it for stabling their horses and fired hundreds of bullets into the wooden angels soaring high among the rafters. Yet it has survived, and still displays such charming features as the carved poppy-heads of the pews which portray the seven deadly sins in a manner instantly intelligible to ordinary folk. Slander has a long sharp tongue; Sloth is a man sitting in bed; and Drunkenness shows the miscreant as an object of ridicule with his feet locked in the village stocks.

Blythburgh's church is thus defiantly intact but the fate of **St Andrew's, Walberswick** and **St Andrew's, Covehithe** has been less fortunate. In the former, a tiny part of the original church has been retained as a parish church but the rest is a ruinous shell. In the latter, a similar spectacle awaits: the parish church is a humble thatched barn of a building, parked like a caretaker's hut in what was once the nave of a mighty church. The tower and walls of the fifteenth-century church are officially redundant, but services are regularly held in the smaller edifice which was built in 1672 mainly of plundered stone. It is possible that the church was out of all proportion to the population of the locality even when it was first built and that it was a pious *folie de largesse* of the wealthy cleric William Yarmouth.

The road to Norwich now beckons, but a brief detour will take in that bizarre lakeland known as the **Norfolk Broads**. These quarter of a million acres of lakes, now interconnected by canals, are no freak of nature but the indirect result of medieval enterprise. The cutting of millions of peat turves for household fuel over the centuries carved great holes in the ground. Already in the fourteenth century there was occasional inundation, but rising sea levels brought about the permanent flooding of the diggings; and by the end of the Middle Ages the process was completed.

LOOKS CAN DECEIVE. *Like many English cathedrals, that at Norwich is not quite what it seems at first glance. The graceful spire and vault sit on robust Norman arcading.*

Much of the peat would have been consumed in the regional capital of **Norwich**, the largest centre of population of East Anglia then as now. There was already a sizeable town here when the Normans implanted their castle which was followed by the cathedral priory. The keep of **Norwich Castle** still stands on its mound hard by the Market Place. The cosmetic neatness of the exterior is the result of a face-lift with Bath stone carried out by that great restorer Anthony Salvin in the 1830s. A more accurate idea of the powerful Norman masonry may be gained from the smoke-blackened interior. The building of the castle was at the expense of some 100 houses of the Saxon town. Further disruption was caused by the establishment of **Norwich Cathedral** and its priory in 1096 by Bishop Herbert de Losinga, a vast project which swallowed up the palace of the former Saxon Earl of East Anglia.

Popular resentment of the Normans simmered on as more and more privileges were granted to the newcomers. Feelings against the monks ran particularly high, but it was not until 1272 that the pot finally came to the boil with an urban riot and the burning of the monastic precincts by the angry townsfolk. After order had been restored, the citizens were obliged to contribute forced labour as a penance on the construction of the principal entrance to the Cathedral Close, the **Ethelbert Gate**. It seems hardly credible, as one strolls through the elegant gatehouse into this most tranquil of ecclesiastical enclaves, to imagine this place as a scene of violence. The other gate to the Close, the **Erpingham Gate**, was the personal endowment of Sir Thomas Erpingham in 1420. This veteran of Agincourt is also remembered for his brief appearance in Shakespeare's *Henry V*, whom the King addresses:

> Good morrow, old Sir Thomas Erpingham.
> A good soft pillow for that good white head
> Were better than a churlish turf of France.

The statue of the old warrior may be seen in a niche above the archway.

The Close itself is like a garden city within the city, a walled enclosure like a jealously guarded piece of paradise. As if to emphasise the point, Norwich's oldest pub, the Adam and Eve, is located just outside the walls of the Close.

The Cathedral itself is a happy blend of Norman robustness in the arcading of the nave, transepts and choir and Perpendicular bravado in the roof of intricate lierne vaulting of the fifteenth century. The composition is crowned by a graceful spire, second in height only to that of Salisbury. Inside, there is an ambulatory behind the high altar and the bishop's throne which occupies a commanding position in the apse. Beneath the bishop's throne there is a curious small recess. This once housed some holy relics; apparently, the idea of the contrivance was that the divine essence of the relics could ascend through a flue and give holy inspiration to the bishop sitting on the throne above. In today's climate which tends to view all religious phenomena solely as spiritual symbols, it is useful to be reminded that medieval faith was unencumbered by such notions. Miracles were held to be physical realities which belonged to the everyday world: and even heavenly grace could be channelled through a conduit of stone.

Re-emerging from the Cathedral Close through the Ethelbert Gate, there is that sinister-sounding area of Tombland to be crossed. Although highly suggestive of a mass burial pit from the Black Death, the name is in fact derived from Danish and signifies nothing more than 'open ground', for this was the Saxon marketplace of Norwich, overlooked by the palace of the Earl of East Anglia. From here, a maze of medieval streets extend their tentacles and create a period atmosphere of great charm. **Elm Hill** is the most famous of these ancient thoroughfares, although only one of its buildings escaped the disastrous fire of 1507. Looking up Elm Hill the vista is focused on the noble east window of **Blackfriars Hall**, once the chancel of the friary church. Together with the adjoining **St Andrew's Hall** and associated cloisters this complex amounts to the largest surviving Dominican establishment in England.

The extent of Norwich's medieval heritage may be gauged by the number of its parish churches within the walls. Some thirty-one of these delightful churches, displaying an amazing degree of homogeneity through the ubiquitous use of knapped flint combined with stone, mark the position of the small urban parishes. They range from the humble **St Etheldreda** to the majestic **St Peter Mancroft** which looms large over the Market Place. The east window of St Peter Mancroft is one of the glories of medieval Norwich, a huge tableau of fifteenth-century glass presenting a picture book of light and colour that could be easily read by the congregation of the day. On the other side of the Market Place, the **Guildhall** has undergone much conversion and modification as a working building, but it manages to convey a hybrid medieval impression. Isolated stretches of Norwich's circuit of city walls may still be followed, and among a wealth of secular building there is **Strangers Hall**, originally a merchant's house of the fourteenth century, which owes its name to its use in the sixteenth century as a staging post for the foreign weavers brought over to revive Norwich's flagging worsted manufacture. Another glimpse into Norwich's commercial past may be obtained at the **Dragon Hall** in King Street. This fifteenth-century merchant's establishment was built as a cloth showroom by one Robert Toppes, four times Lord Mayor of Norwich and the city's burgess in Parliament. Its present name comes from the discovery beneath layers of plaster of a beautifully carved and painted dragon, one of several which once adorned the spandrels of the open timber roof.

Finally, to pluck one last blossom from the orchard – and an anonymous nineteenth-century source described Norwich as a 'city in an orchard' – we proceed down St Julian's Alley off King Street to the **Church of St Julian**. The Norman church was severely bombed during the war and has been entirely rebuilt; but this was the site of the cell of the fourteenth-century anchoress and mystic Dame Julian of Norwich, whose *Revelations of Divine Love* was a medieval bestseller and qualifies her as the first known woman writer to be published in England. Her cell has been reconstructed on its medieval foundation and is attracting a growing pilgrimage traffic.

FOR SERVICES RENDERED. *This is how the crafty lawyer John Heydon might well have viewed his acquisition of Baconsthorpe Castle in Norfolk. His once noble residence later became a sheep farm and centre for cloth manufacture.*

DECLINE AND FALL. *This has been the fate of Walsingham since the Dissolution of the Monasteries. The recent revival of pilgrimage traffic has done much to restore the fortunes of this small town in north Norfolk.*

Scant remains of North Elmham's cathedral.

The onward journey into rural Norfolk can be pursued on any number of deserted country lanes as haphazard in their course as the cracks in the glaze of old porcelain. It seems that each individual farm created its own track to the nearest village and followed field boundaries rather than the most direct route. This maze of a landscape stretches out under the broadest sky to be found in England; it is studded by grey flint towers of the churches which provide the perfect foil to the yellow corn, green meadows and red-brick houses. This is not a country rich in memories of great battles and heroic events but an altogether quieter place. Yet, as the labyrinth of ancient roads proclaims, the area was more densely populated in the Middle Ages than today, and it conceals some surprising vestiges of the period.

Excavations in 1903 in the sleepy village of **North Elmham** revealed the foundations of a Saxon cathedral beneath the ruins of a moated castle. North Elmham was the seat of the Bishops of Norfolk from the late seventh century until the Viking raids began in earnest. Then about 955 there was a church here for the re-established seat of a bishopric covering the whole of East Anglia, and it is these remains which can be seen today. The bishopric was moved to Thetford in about 1072 for a brief while before finding its permanent home in Norwich in the 1090s. North Elmham remained in the possession of the Bishops of Norwich, and it was one of their number, Henry le Despenser, appointed in 1370, who converted the former cathedral and burial ground into a moated hunting lodge; for the chase rather than the cross was this man's true vocation. Archaeologists have unearthed evidence of another of Bishop Henry's earthly passions: huge quantities of drinking horns and jugs suggest some riotous living after the excitement of the hunt. After Henry le Despenser's death in 1406 this pleasure lodge was abandoned and fell into ruins.

Some distance to the north lie the better preserved remains of **Baconsthorpe Castle**, still moated and in a mysterious way more enchanting than many a grander castle. This late fifteenth-century stronghold was the work of John Heydon, who earned himself the reputation of a cunning lawyer who made his fortune during the Wars of the Roses by profiting from the misfortunes of others. In the relatively secure climate of the Tudor era John Heydon's descendants converted the family home into a sheep farm which catered for all stages of wool processing to the weaving of the cloth.

Walsingham's medieval prosperity sprang from that other lucrative business, pilgrimage traffic. During the period of its glory from the early twelfth century until the Dissolution the Shrine of Our Lady of Walsingham was internationally renowned and came second only to that of St Thomas in Canterbury for the number of pilgrims it attracted from home and abroad. Erasmus paid a visit to Walsingham in 1511 and noted that this was 'a town maintained by scarcely anything else but the number of its visitors'. The same may be said today.

The miracle that transformed Walsingham into a major shrine occurred around 1100 when Richelde of Fervaques had a dream in which she was taken to the house in Nazareth where the Virgin Mary received the Annunciation of Christ's birth from the Archangel Gabriel. Richelde was directed in the dream to build a replica of the Holy House in Walsingham. She had it built of wood near two wells, but by some heavenly intervention it was whisked away one night to a site about 200 feet distant. This was enough to confirm its sanctity, and the pilgrims began to arrive. By 1153 an Augustinian priory was established at Walsingham, and an active promotion of the Holy House was commenced. As with other more recent tourism successes the seal of royal approval made a tremendous impact: Henry III made frequent pilgrimages and his son Edward I visited Walsingham in 1281 just after the new church was constructed.

A sure sign of bulging coffers was the complete rebuilding of the church and priory in the fourteenth century. Despite the protests of the Augustinians, the Franciscans founded a friary in Walsingham. It is not recorded if this syphoned off some of the pilgrimage receipts from the priory as had been feared. In any case, there is every indication that the Augustinians continued to thrive right into the sixteenth century. At the time of the visit by Erasmus in 1511 a new chapel was under construction, and – as Erasmus pointedly observed – the Holy House had been repaired and restored to such an extent that most of its material was new. On the eve of the Dissolution Walsingham was, after Norwich, the second wealthiest monastery in Norfolk. An ill-advised conspiracy to thwart the will of Henry VIII led to the brutal execution of the Prior George Gysburghe and the Sub-Prior Nicholas Mileham before the Priory was officially surrendered on 4 August 1538. The ensuing destruction was almost total. All that remains today is the stately east end of the church and part of the refectory. The miraculous Holy House has vanished without a trace.

LIGHT AND SHADE. *The play of sunshine across the entrance to the keep at Castle Rising in Norfolk adds substantially to the drama of the ascending staircase.*

BRIDGE TO NOWHERE. *The triangular bridge at Crowland in Lincolnshire originally spanned three streams of the River Welland, now re-routed. The structure survives as a curiosity; the statue is thought to have been taken from the nearby abbey.*

The church of St Margaret, King's Lynn.

For centuries Walsingham was expunged from the religious map until a private initiative in 1896 led to the rehabilitation of the Shrine of Our Lady. In 1897 the so-called Slipper Chapel was rebuilt, its name referring to the medieval custom of pilgrims leaving their footwear here in order to walk the last mile or so of their journey barefoot. Walsingham is now shared by Anglicans, Catholics and Methodists; and even the Russian Orthodox Church in Exile has set up a chapel under a characteristic onion-shaped dome in the building of the redundant railway station.

The influence of the Bishop of Norwich may be felt as far west as **King's Lynn** which was founded in 1101 by the same Herbert de Losinga who began the construction of Norwich Cathedral. This strategic seaport where the Fenland meets the Wash more than fulfilled the bishop's expectations and flourished throughout the Middle Ages. The old town is still markedly medieval in layout; and the Tuesday Market Place and the Saturday Market Place are the dominant features even today. By the latter, St Margaret's Church and the fifteenth-century Town Hall are the main buildings of the period. Near by, a cobbled alleyway leads down to the South Quay. Centuries ago this would have been a narrow canal giving access to the imposing range of Hanseatic Warehouses which were built in about 1475 as the specific local depot for trade with the great merchant cities of northern Germany. Though but a stone's throw from the waterfront, these buildings have lost their own private lifeline to the sea and serve as yet another poignant reminder of the receding tide of international commerce.

Across the flat Fenland, at the small market town of **March** the church of **St Wendreda** contains one of the most crowded angel roofs in the country. There is scarcely a free spot for another of these carved beauties to perch. An enigmatic piece of architecture awaits at **Crowland**. Right in the middle of the town stands a triangular bridge of the fourteenth century, whose arches once spanned the three separate streams of the River Welland. Sadly, the water has been diverted so that this unique structure now appears like some forgotten folly, bereft of any practical purpose. A carved seated figure of regal bearing adorns one arm of the bridge. This is most probably a statue of Christ taken from **Crowland Abbey** which is famed for the sculptural elegance of its west front and is the reputed burial place of Hereward the Wake, the last leader of the Saxon resistance to the Normans, who met his end in 1071 among the marshy wastes near Ely.

Peterborough Cathedral, with its magnificent Early English west front and Perpendicular tower dominates its city, but there is a lesser known medieval jewel on the outskirts of Peterborough at **Longthorpe Tower**. This crenellated tower, built around 1300 by Robert Thorpe, boasts the best preserved and most extensive set of medieval wall paintings yet to be found in England. The subject matter is allegorical and Biblical, depicting scenes such as the Nativity and King David playing the harp, but other, fresher images crowd in with birds and flowers, musicians and heraldic devices to make Longthorpe Tower's Great Chamber an eye-dazzling experience. Elsewhere, neglect and vandalism have combined to eradicate all but the faintest trace of domestic mural paintings, so that we are liable to receive a false impression of medieval interiors as blank walls with perhaps the occasional tapestry. The reality, as Longthorpe Tower shows, was rather different: the homes of the well-to-do were alive with colour and beguiling images.

The lofty octagonal lantern of **Ely Cathedral** is an imposing landmark for miles around, soaring high above the flat Cambridgeshire countryside. By virtue of its proximity it serves as a curtain-raiser to the architectural marvels of Cambridge. But it is worth resisting the lure of the ancient university to sample Ely's relative calm, for this is a city that has been largely bypassed by the developments of the industrial age. It is also of interest to stop at **Denny Abbey** which lies directly on the road to Cambridge. From the outside it presents itself as a substantial farmhouse, but an inspection of the inside reveals that this was once a church of the Benedictines that was later adapted by the Knights Templar and a community of Franciscan nuns, each in their turn. This is truly a building that has lived many separate lives in the course of its 800 years of service.

Cambridge is of course as an institution a still-living link with medieval England; and it is striking to note the extent to which the university has dictated the urban plan. In contrast to Oxford, there appears to be little space for a commercial sector; the few shops in the centre of the city seem to have elbowed themselves painfully into very narrow plots, while the great colleges sprawl majestically as if land was a limitless commodity. The Great Court at Trinity could easily accommodate several football pitches, and it takes only a light mist to drift in from the Fens to obscure one side from the other. **King's College Chapel** enjoys the most generous of settings; and its ethereal beauty can be enjoyed from many vantage points. This building marks the high tide of Perpendicular Gothic which reaches a natural finale in the supreme elegance of fan-vaulting and windows so vast that the delicate masonry might seem to be in danger of simply floating away. After this, there was really no way forward for the Gothic style; and it is not surprising that, after a respectful interval, architects and builders tried something completely different with the rediscovered forms of Classical antiquity delivered by the Renaissance.

As a living city, Cambridge has never stopped rebuilding, so that much of its original medieval character has been replaced and upstaged by Tudor, Jacobean and Georgian. The parts still most redolent of the Middle Ages are to be found in quiet corners such as the **Old**

WOOL WEALTH. *Suffolk's churches owe much to the munificence of the local merchants. An angel roof at Blythburgh* (right), *and the splendid new fabric at Long Melford* (above), *are the fruit of commercial patronage.*

Lavenham's Guildhall – tour de force *of medieval carpentry.*

Court of Corpus Christi, which claims to be the oldest college quadrangle in England, dating back to about 1350. At **Queens' College** we have an early example of brick building from the mid fifteenth century which has much in common with some of the larger manorial homes of the period.

Nowadays, London is only an hour away from Cambridge, but another detour is called for to take in **Bury St Edmunds**, where a plaque in the abbey ruins informs that this place was the real cradle of English democracy, since it was here that the rebellious barons first drew up their constitutional demands which were later incorporated into the Magna Carta.

From Bury St Edmunds the delightful Suffolk countryside extends to the south; its church towers and half-timbered villages supply all the cosy images of rural England. Yet this was the scene of England's first industrial revolution, that of organised wool production and cloth manufacture in the Middle Ages. It is above all at **Lavenham** that the vestiges of that activity may be most keenly felt. The town possesses not just individual buildings of the Middle Ages but entire streetscapes which would still be familiar to the inhabitants of almost 500 years ago. The **Guildhall** commands the whole south side of the town's marketplace, a glorious, rambling half-timbered building which played a central role in civic life as well as providing a scenic backdrop for the pageantry and festivals such as the great procession to mark the feast of Corpus Christi on the Thursday after Trinity Sunday.

The role of the guilds in Suffolk was by no means exclusively economic. Indeed, their prime objects were social and religious, with the dispensing of charity to the poor and the endowment of chantries and churches. Lavenham once had four separate guildhalls; and the **Guild of Our Lady** still stands at the bottom of Lady Street. In Water Street a row of cottages known as the Flemish Weavers' stand in memory of the countless skilled workers who came to Lavenham from Flanders and gave the local industry the benefit of their labour and talents. Today there is no longer the sound of looms at work in the weavers' cottages; and a sweet silence hangs over the town, once one of the busiest and richest in England.

But the greatest and most enduring monument to Suffolk's woolmen and clothiers, spinners and weavers, are the churches. The profits of the commerce were poured into lavish building projects of staggering scale and beauty. Church towers, lofty naves with broad expanses of magical stained glass and timber roofs with carved angels arose as vibrant symbols of a deeply felt faith and a common purpose. These 'wool churches' were built in the Perpendicular style, and they are still the principal adornment of the region. Among the many fine examples, **Lavenham's St Peter and St Paul** vies with **Long Melford's Holy Trinity** for the top prize. The stained glass at Long Melford is one of the glories of the age; but it is above all the light and spaciousness of these churches which remains in the mind. They create a scale and harmony where human beings may feel inspired without being intimidated. And that was the spiritual climate which was evolving as the Middle Ages matured slowly but surely towards the intellectual liberation of the Renaissance.

Stanway in Gloucestershire – a fleeting glimpse of the Middle Ages.

IV. THAMES VALLEY AND THE COTSWOLDS

RAVELLERS HEADING WEST from London along the M4 motorway can enjoy a spectacular, albeit distant view, of what appears to be a complete fortified city of the Middle Ages. A dramatic composition of walls, bastions, towers and battlements rises high over the Thames Valley, asserting an ancient authority over what must be one of the most developed corners of England. However, **Windsor Castle** is not, on closer inspection, quite what it pretends to be; for its 'medieval' skyline dates back no further than the early nineteenth century, when George IV and his architect Jeffrey Wyatville radically remodelled the incoherent cluster of buildings which had accumulated here by a process of accretion almost, since the time of William the Conqueror. The true architectural history of Windsor Castle would involve a lengthy roll call of English monarchy from Henry II to Charles II, but the overall effect of picturesque pastiche is the legacy of George IV.

There is, however, one authentic medieval gem to be admired at Windsor in the splendid **St George's Chapel**. This glorious expression of the Perpendicular style was commenced in 1475 by Edward IV, who is buried here beneath a simple slab of black marble, as the spiritual headquarters and shrine of the Order of the Garter, originally founded by Edward III more than a century earlier. The choir of St George's Chapel encapsulates perfectly the spirit of the age when knightly display and pageantry had become more important than the inner essence of chivalry. The two ranges of the Garter Stalls, carved between 1478–85, face each other across a paved aisle, beneath which are the funeral vaults of later kings. The intricate carpentry of the Garter Stalls is covered with a riot of heraldic decoration with banners, helms and crests rampant above a colourful patchwork of painted coats of arms and other knightly insignia. This is the very stuff of which today's perception of medieval courtly society is made.

Windsor Castle, for all its splendour and royal pedigree, exudes an unreal quality which derives from the curious combination of genuine medieval content and the nineteenth-century revival of the Middle Ages. Here the two have merged together imperceptibly and present themselves as a homogeneous piece of British heritage. The ambivalence has much to do with the march of history which has conserved the institution of the monarchy while

Key

Cathedral

Church or Chapel

Abbey or Priory

Castle

Notable building(s) or structure(s)

Burford
Minster Lovell
Witney
Oxford

OXFORDSHIRE

R. Thames or Isis
R. Thame
Abingdon
Faringdon
Great Coxwell
Vale of the White Horse
Wantage
Dorchester
Ewelme
Wallingford
High Wycombe

BUCKINGHAM~SHIRE

R. Thames
Maidenhead
Eton
Windsor

BERKSHIRE

R. Thames
Reading

Peter McClure 1990

Great Malvern
R. Avon
Evesham

HEREFORD & WORCESTER

Hereford
Ledbury
Chipping Campden

R. Wye
Kilpeck
Tewkesbury
Deerhurst
Stanway
Hailes Abbey
Sudeley Castle

Abbey Dore
Ross-on-Wye
Cheltenham

WALES
Goodrich

GLOUCESTER~SHIRE

R. Wye
Gloucester
Cotswold Hills
Northleach

River Severn
Stroud
Cirencester
Fairford

Berkeley

0   5   10   15 km
0   5   10 miles

modifying substantially its role in the life of the nation. The fabric of Windsor, for all its artfulness and historicism, is an authentic reflection of that process, living history in the true sense of the expression.

From the ramparts of Windsor Castle the view encompasses another medieval relic which is also a great national institution. **Eton College** was founded in 1440 by Henry VI in order to provide a fitting education for seventy poor scholars. Today, there are still seventy scholars at Eton, not many of them very poor, but they are outnumbered by some 1200 so-called Oppidans. As for the school, it does incorporate a great deal of medieval fabric. The chapel of 1441–61 is essentially just the choir of what was intended to be a much larger foundation. An air raid in 1940 destroyed its medieval stained glass and the modern replacements, whatever their intrinsic artistic merit, do little justice to their host windows. It comes also as a shock to learn that the roof of the chapel is a blatant sham, being an imitation of fan-vaulting composed of stone-faced concrete mounted on steel supports. Lack of money had dictated that the original roof was made of wood rather than stone, and the usual problems of dry rot and attack by beetle eventually took their toll. On the positive side, the chapel contains some remarkable late fifteenth-century wall paintings, which were discovered beneath a layer of plaster in 1923.

For many scholars of Eton down the ages it was the road to Oxford, an even more ancient seat of learning, that beckoned. The road thither follows the Thames Valley and crosses the river at Henley. Just before Wallingford, a handsome market town of Saxon origins, a meandering country lane leads to the village of **Ewelme**. Here, a scene is to be encountered which is still as medieval at heart as that described by John Leland some 450 years ago:

> Ewelme paroche chirche a cumly and new peace of work standing on an hille was lately made by William Duke of Southfolk and Alice his wife. William was slayn, and Alice supervivid, and after was byried yn the paroche chirch of Ewelme on the south side of the high altare in a rich tumbe of alabastre, with an image in the habite of a woves crounid lying over it . . . . The pratie hospital of poore men is hard joynid to the west ende of Ewelm paroche chirch . . . and in the middle of the area of the hospitale is a very fair welle.

And so it all remains to this day. But one salient point should be added: beneath the sumptuous alabaster effigy of Alice de la Pole, Duchess of Suffolk, and half hidden behind some Gothic stone tracery, may be espied a naturalistic carving in miniature of the cadaver of an old woman, gaunt and emaciated. Death, we are hereby reminded in characteristic medieval fashion, is physical decomposition as well as spiritual transformation. The magical peace of the almshouses huddled around their courtyard and overlooked by the protective tower of the church, quickly dispels such brutal images with its implicit message of community and continuity through the ages. The well mentioned by Leland is located in the middle of the quadrangle. The Ewelme spring had previously been celebrated in verse by Geoffrey Chaucer no less:

THE AGONY AND THE ECSTASY. *Both aspects of death are present in the tomb of Alice de la Pole at Ewelme in Oxfordshire. Beneath the sublime effigy there lies a grotesque cadaver in miniature.*

'THE PRATIE HOSPITAL OF POORE MEN.' *John Leland's description of the Ewelme almhouses in the 1530s is still accurate. This is one of the most satisfying enclaves of medieval England.*

In worlde is none more clere of hue,
Its water ever fresshe and newe,
That whelmeth up in waves bright
The mountance of three fingers height.

A bit closer towards Oxford lies the town of **Dorchester**, once prosperous on account of its abbey of Augustinian monks, founded in 1140. The abbey church was transferred to parochial use at the Dissolution and was thereby spared the destruction of those times. Leland mentions in some detail the fine medieval effigies lying in the abbey church. One in particular caught his imagination; and he described it as follows: 'There be buried in the quier beside divers abbates a knight on the south side with an image crosse leggid, whos name is there oute of remembrance.' The powerful and dynamic effigy of the nameless knight is a fine specimen of funerary sculpture in action rather than repose. In fact, nothing could be further from the meek acceptance of death common to most memorials than this carving of a medieval warrior, frozen in the act of drawing his sword from its scabbard. Dated to around 1300, the effigy appears to express in symbolic form the undaunted spirit of the True Crusader, fighting on even from beyond the grave for a cause that was already doomed to failure.

Oxford, despite its many fine Classical and modern buildings, still presents us with an overwhelmingly medieval experience. The heart of the city has been taken up by the various colleges which have expanded remorselessly at the expense of the town, enclosing acre upon acre behind high walls and forbidding gatehouses, each one a self-contained community. The whole scheme of things may best be appreciated from one of Oxford's lofty vantage points such as Carfax Tower or the tower of St Mary the Virgin. A patchwork of green squares, the college quadrangles, held together by a limestone labyrinth of cloisters and passages connecting chapels, dining halls and residential blocks, unfolds into the distance. Occasional larger expanses of green, mostly of irregular shape, are the college gardens. The pattern owes much to the monastic establishments which preceded the University as such.

Surprisingly, only one of Oxford's many monastic and friary churches has survived, that of the Priory of St Frideswide, a mighty Norman structure which now forms the nave, crossing and choir arcade of the **Cathedral Church of Christ**, which by a quirk of ecclesiastical history constitutes an integral part of Christ Church College. The choir is particularly splendid: the muscular Norman work supports a most graceful and intricate lierne vault of the late fifteenth century.

But the serious medievalist had better beware of surface impressions in Oxford, for the taste for Gothic never really disappeared and there is much pseudo-Gothic spanning the centuries from the waning of the Middle Ages to the full-blooded Gothic Revival of the nineteenth century. **New College** conveys an authentic feel of the early medieval period; its foundation in 1379 marked the definitive step in formalising the concept of the Oxford college as a self-regulating residential body. It also gave expression to the architectural scheme of the cloistered quadrangle which was much taken up elsewhere. In the chapel of New College there is a delightful fourteenth-century carved misericord portraying a book carrier. Books were heavy as well as precious, and it was common practice for a scout to carry the fellow's books to lectures. The location of New College hard by the north-east sector of the city wall brought with it the obligation to maintain this part of Oxford's defences. This obligation has been effectively honoured, for the boundary of

Merton College, Oxford.

the college garden is still marked by the original city wall, complete with medieval bastions.

Another large stretch of wall runs along the north side of Christ Church Meadow. Behind it there shelters one of Oxford's most ancient enclaves. **Merton College**, founded in 1264, boasts the oldest college buildings of the University; its Mob Quad claims to be the earliest quadrangle, but it evolved piecemeal rather than as a preconceived planning proposition. The upper floor library, designed to keep the damp away from the parchment, dates back to 1373–8 and is the oldest library in the country. Although its shelves were refitted in 1623, it still displays its leather-bound tomes on shelves equipped with the fittings for the chaining of books, a common medieval practice which in Oxford lasted well into the eighteenth century. Merton also gave Oxford the prototype of the college chapel: a truncated building, restricted in space, consisting of choir and antechapel. The marvellous pinnacled tower of the mid-fifteenth century sits rather low, considering its noble girth, but this makes it a more intimate sight than many a lofty spire.

So inextricably is the idea of Oxford bound up with the University that the town itself is easily overlooked. The commercial centre is crowded into the western part of the city, where

THE BODY IN THE WALL. *The romantic ruins of Minster Lovell Hall on the banks of the River Windrush seem an unlikely spot for the macabre discovery of a corpse in the masonry. This was once the ancestral home of the Lords Lovell.*

ARCHITECTURAL IMPROVISATION. *The proliferation of chapels in varying styles of Gothic at the east end of Cirencester church shows the relaxed medieval attitude towards existing buildings. Organic growth rather than stylistic purity was the norm.*

the castle once stood. Marooned behind a modern shopping centre like an obscure object of shame, stands the huge 'motte' or mound – all that remains of the castle. St George's Tower, within the castle precinct, now occupied by HM Prison, maintains a furtive watch over the waters of what was once the mill stream. The late Saxon tower of **St Michael** marks the site of the North Gate in Cornmarket, and forms a picturesque group with the adjacent timber-framed town house of about 1470.

The condominium of Town and Gown was often troubled during the Middle Ages. The influx of so many students, as hot-blooded then as now, led to violent clashes with the youth of the town. The notorious riots of 1209, 1298 and 1355 were but the highlights of a long-running conflict of interests. As Leland informs us, the University and its ancillary services already dominated Oxford as early as the thirteenth century: 'The toune of Oxford moste floryshed withe scollars in an huge nombar, and other inhabitaunts in Henry the 3. tyme. Ther was an infinit nombar of writers and parchement makers in Oxford . . .' Recent archaeology is redressing the balance, showing that medieval Oxford was also a notable centre of commerce in its own right and once boasted a Norman bridge with houses and shops which preceded that of London by some eighty years.

The abiding attraction of Oxford's medieval heritage is the way it effortlessly pervades the fabric of modern life. Ancient buildings still serve their time-hallowed purpose; and others such as the twelfth-century parish church of **St Peter-in-the-East**, now converted into the college library of St Edmund Hall, have found a new lease of life. Even behind the neo-Classical façade of **Worcester College** we encounter a range of humble medieval lodgings squaring up to their stately neighbours of eighteenth-century elegance across the lawn, in no way upstaged by the juxtaposition. Such effects are only possible because the spirit of the place is faithful to its medieval roots. The colleges with their halls and chapels are the living cells of Oxford today; and there is no sense of any anachronism in the co-existence of old and new. The fortunate Fellows of Merton may promenade in their private garden along the ramparts of the old city wall and enjoy a secret world that is both medieval and modern at the same time.

Minster Lovell, an enchanting ruined manor house several miles out of town in rural Oxfordshire, may serve to underline the fact that, for all of Oxford's wisdom and wit, it was still the land-owning knightly class which formed the backbone of England throughout the Middle Ages. This was the ancestral home of the Lords Lovell, a line which was extinguished under uncertain circumstances. William Camden, the sixteenth-century antiquarian, records that 'Francis Viscount Lovel Lord Chamberlain to King Richard 3. who was banisht by Henry 7. and at last slain in the battle of Stoke, taking part with Lambert the imposter Prince.' Another version of the sad end of the family saga has Francis, 9th Baron Lovell, going into hiding within the vaults of Minster Lovell after taking part in the unsuccessful revolt against Henry VII in 1487. The reported discovery of a man's skeleton walled up in a secret chamber, which came to light in 1708, gave added substance to the latter version. But such sinister happenings seem out of character with this idyllic spot beside the River Windrush, as this upper tributary of the Isis and the Thames is known. The building remains consist of the fifteenth-century hall and porch of an imposing manorial home. In the nearby church reposes a fine alabaster effigy of a medieval knight. Although without any inscription, it has been identified from the style of its armour and heraldic devices as being a likeness of William Lovell (1397–1455), one of the last of the Lords Lovell of Minster of the old creation.

Great Coxwell, the most acclaimed barn in England.

Before heading further west into the Cotswolds, it is worth making the southerly detour to the tiny village of **Great Coxwell** near Faringdon to admire a building of the highest distinction. Erected around the middle of the thirteenth century by the Cistercians, this magnificent tithe barn of limestone walls and oak roof has withstood the ravages of wind and weather for over 700 years. Its powerful simplicity and graceful engineering endow it with a quality every bit as awe-inspiring as that of a Gothic cathedral. Note the holes under the eaves of the east gable forming the most stylish of dovecotes.

The Cotswolds are still one of the great wool-producing regions of England. In the Middle Ages they were pre-eminent, as expressed in a rhyme which must rank as a medieval publicity slogan:

> In Europe the best wool is English.
> In England, the best wool is the Cotswold.

The Cotswolds, a range of limestone hills whose name signifies 'sheepfold on the hill', are also famous for their honey-coloured building stone which has been quarried over the centuries to provide the material for scores of manors and churches, and hundreds of cottages and farms liberally scattered over the undulating countryside. The architectural

CRIME AND PUNISHMENT. *The horrific assassination of Edward II at Berkeley Castle* (left) *led to the erection of a magnificent shrine in Gloucester Cathedral. Pilgrims' donations financed a lavish rebuilding which included the fan-vaulted lavatorium* (above).

quality of these structures is tangible evidence of the great wealth that was carried on the sheep's back.

Fairford, Gloucestershire, was one of the leading wool towns of the Cotswolds; and it owed much to the enterprise and generosity of a family called Tame. According to John Leland, 'Fairford never florishid afore the coming of the Tames onto it. John Tame began the fair new church of Fairforde, and Edmund Tame finishid it. Both John and Edmund ly buried in a chapelle of the north side of Fairford quier.' There they lie today: the memorial brass on the Purbeck marble tomb of John Tame also depicts his wife Alice who died prematurely in 1471, leaving her husband to survive her for a long twenty-nine years. But the church at Fairford is chiefly renowned for its twenty-eight windows of stained glass, dating from around 1500. Despite some losses and restoration, they represent the most complete set of medieval glass of any parish church in England. The vibrant colours of the Middle Ages speak of an unalloyed delight in bold hues and rich effects. The majestic tower and noble proportions of the nave rank St Mary, Fairford, very high on any architectural listing.

Northleach tells a similar tale of a rich clothier pouring the profits of trade into the embellishment of the parish church. Here, it was John Fortey who provided the cash for the clerestory over the chancel and much else besides. He died in 1458 and is commemorated in a brass portrait which shows him with one foot on a sheep and the other on a woolsack. There are several other memorial brasses to other clothiers bearing similar insignia. That of John Taylor displays a woolmark composed of two shepherd's crooks forming a cross. Incidentally, the clothiers of Northleach were proud of the fact that an Italian merchant Francesco Datini took the trouble to record that 'the finest and most expensive wool was the English which came from Chondisgualdo (Cotswolds) and in particular from Norleccio (Northleach) . . . and the great abbey lands of Siricestri (Cirencester)'.

Cirencester in its previous existence as Roman Corinium was once the second city of Britannia and it still enjoys the honorary rank and title of 'Capital of the Cotswolds'. The present market town grew up around the great abbey founded by Henry I in 1117. The church was extensively rebuilt in the fourteenth and fifteenth centuries, and its most striking feature is the three-storey porch overlooking the marketplace. It was added in around 1490 to provide a place for the conduct of secular business. So convenient were the meeting facilities it offered that it came to be used after the Dissolution as the Town Hall of Cirencester. Although the south porch was officially made over to the parish for church use more than 300 years ago, it is still known by some as the Town Hall.

Where the Cotswolds have run their course and the hills run down towards the mouth of the Severn stands **Berkeley Castle**. Its stone of rose red and grey has been described as having 'the colour of old brocade'. It is a modest fortification as castles go, but it possesses a powerful compactness, clustered tightly around two courtyards. The main entrance from the inner courtyard is decorated with fanciful ogee tracery, and the Great Hall of the 1340s sports the famous five-sided 'Berkeley arches'. But it is not for such refinements that Berkeley Castle is chiefly known. Rather, it owes its fame or notoriety to the foul murder committed here in 1327 of King Edward II at the instigation of his Queen Isabella and her lover Roger Mortimer. Yet it is not the mere fact of regicide which has etched the name of Berkeley into history's inventory of assassinations but the brutal manner in which the monarch was ultimately despatched.

At first, it was attempted to kill Edward by asphyxiation. A deep hole in one corner of the room where he was confined goes down far into the foundations of the castle where a charnel well, stuffed with the rotting corpses of many animals, exuded its deadly stench of putrefaction. When this 'natural' method failed, Edward's jailors Sir John Matravers and Sir Thomas Gurney devised something infinitely more fiendish. The room may still be seen where the murderers held down their victim and tried to stifle his screams as they forced red-hot irons into his bowels. This was done, so it is said, in order to leave no traces of assault on the corpse; but it smacks more of medieval barbarism and gratuitous sadism.

If the aim was to pass off Edward's death as being from natural causes, then the scheme went hopelessly wrong. The sheer horror of the deed has been remembered to this day in the dramatic words of Christopher Marlowe: 'The shrieks of death through Berkeley's roof that ring. Shrieks of an agonising king.' Edward II was ceremoniously interred in **Gloucester Cathedral**, and the funeral procession must have followed the old road overlaid by the modern A38. By way of compensation for his torment, or so it might seem, Edward II was commemorated with a monument which ranks as one of the extravaganzas of medieval design. The tombchest of Purbeck marble with ogee-arched recesses supports the alabaster effigy of ethereal expression, carved by London craftsmen around 1330. Above it a lofty and intricate canopy of Cotswold limestone rises in two stages, amounting to a work of architecture in its own right. Sympathy for the suffering of the king was so intense that his tomb rapidly became a shrine and an object of popular veneration. It attracted countless pilgrims, and their donations provided the means for the great rebuilding of Gloucester Cathedral which took place by the fifteenth century.

Thus it was that the Benedictine Abbey of St Peter, as the church was then known, acquired around its solid Norman heart a magnificent outer shell of the finest Perpendicular Gothic. The new fabric is noted for its great east window, a miraculous expanse of glass, and for the very earliest appearance in England of the new technique of fan-vaulting in the cloister. The daring intricacy of the fan-vault was even extended to the *lavatorium* or washing place of the monks who occupied the abbey until it achieved cathedral status in 1541. Despite its lowly function the *lavatorium* was made beautiful with a range of two-light windows of stained glass to complete one of the most elegant of bathrooms to have been devised.

Gloucester possesses other vestiges of the Middle Ages, but the urban cohesion of the period has been lost since the castle, city walls and gates are no more. However, the

THE POWER OF THE ABBEY. *After the foundation of Tewkesbury Abbey* (above) *the prestige of Deerhurst* (left) *rapidly declined. Modern Tewkesbury is still dominated by its abbey which here overlooks the row of cottages it built as a medieval real-estate venture.*

Naturalistic carving at Deerhurst Church.

Church of the Black Friars remains, together with substantial parts of the domestic buildings, as a rare survival of a Dominican friary. Beneath the pavement outside Boots the Chemist in Eastgate the excavated foundations of both a Roman and a medieval gate are exposed to view. In Northgate there is the galleried courtyard of the **New Inn**, built by the abbey in 1457 to provide lodgings for the pilgrims to the shrine of Edward II. The original timber-framing of the New Inn is essentially intact; and the hostelry still flourishes in continuation of an unbroken medieval tradition.

At this point the ardent medievalist will be amply rewarded by an extension of this journey further west into the Marches to **Goodrich Castle**, the magical Norman church at **Kilpeck**, the ruins of **Abbey Dore**, **Hereford Cathedral** with its Chained Library and the Mappa Mundi and the old town of **Ledbury**.

From Gloucester the main road leads directly to Tewkesbury, but before proceeding to this remarkable ancient town, follow a sign indicating the village of **Deerhurst**. It was at this now obscure location that Canute and Edmund Ironside concluded the treaty which divided England between the Danes and the Saxons. The main reminder here of Saxon times is the church, whose early building history straddles the period from about 790 to 930. It was once the priory church of the most important monastery in the forgotten Saxon kingdom of Hwicce. Much of the Saxon fabric is still strongly in evidence, most obviously the tall, narrow tower with the characteristic irregular quoins known as 'long-and-short' work. There is some splendid Saxon carving both inside and out, including an angel perched high up on the outside wall at the east end. The font is a masterpiece of late ninth-century artistry, the finest of its kind, and there are some authentic Saxon windows and triangular arches. Just a few yards down the lane stands **Odda's Chapel**, simple and austere, dedicated in 1056.

The decline of the priory at Deerhurst was no doubt accelerated by the rise of **Tewkesbury**

Abbey just a few miles away. This great Norman church, founded in 1091, is all that remains of a vast Benedictine monastery, but its mighty tower is by far the most imposing landmark in the town. Tewkesbury has not grown much beyond its medieval layout so that the relationship between the abbey and its surroundings is largely undisturbed. The interior of the abbey shows a familiar blend of uncompromising Norman rotundity and the more intricate vaulting of a later period. Only here the general effect is somewhat marred by the way the new roof cuts across the clerestory, rather like a hat pulled down too low which partially obscures the eyes of the wearer. However, in the choir the marriage of the Norman piers and the Decorated Gothic work of the windows is a much happier arrangement. All this was the gift of Hugh Despenser and his wife Elizabeth Montacute who may be seen in effigy form, lying side by side under a most elaborate canopy of about 1350.

Tewkesbury Abbey offers a fascinating study in posthumous marital relations; for just across the aisle stands the equally splendid monument to Guy de Brien. This was the man that Elizabeth Montacute married after Hugh Despenser's death in 1348. The thrice-married Elizabeth Montacute was buried with her second husband rather than numbers one or three. Guy de Brien took no chances with his own solitary tomb and effigy, for he had them made during his own lifetime and followed the progress of the work with great interest. Note also the kneeling effigy of Edward Despenser to the south: this was a nephew of Hugh, described by the French chronicler Froissart as 'the most honourable, gallant and valliant Knight in all England'. But the funerary monument to beat them all at Tewkesbury was the Beauchamp Chapel, a two-storey affair, crammed with sculpture and two kneeling figures of Isabelle Despenser and her husband called Richard Beauchamp, Earl of Worcester. Isabelle evidently had a taste for husbands called Richard Beauchamp, for she went on to marry the Earl of Warwick of that ilk. But she was buried with her first husband here in Tewkesbury Abbey and not in the even more splendid Beauchamp Chapel in Warwick where her second husband lies in glorious isolation. The Despenser tombs suffered at the hand of the Puritans in the seventeenth century, and the Beauchamp Chapel and the tomb of Hugh Despenser were robbed of their statuary, but what remains still amounts to a most instructive essay on the aristocratic cult of death in the Middle Ages.

In the town of **Tewkesbury** it is hardly possible to avoid seeing the great bulk of the square abbey tower which looms large over the streets and alleyways. Nor is it possible to escape completely the influence of the Benedictine monks, who invested in a shrewd real-estate speculation whose fruits are still with us today in the development known as **Abbey Cottages**. This recently renovated row of combined residential and commercial accommodation in Church Street was completed towards the end of the fifteenth century. These superb examples of late-medieval urban dwellings were equipped with wooden shutters rather than glazed windows; and it is thought that the shutters doubled up as shop counters through the use of a cunning pivot built into the frame. One of the cottages has been reinstated to illustrate the spartan living conditions of the day. The town contains many

FIREPLACE IN THE SKY. *This is how we now experience the former magnificence of the Great Hall at Sudeley Castle. The surviving windows tell of the princely standard of the accommodation.*

HOLY BLOOD. *It was the possession of a phial containing a few drops of Christ's blood which made the fortunes of the Cistercians at Hailes Abbey in Gloucestershire. The ruins have revealed a quite extraordinarily high level of decoration.*

Chipping Campden, viewed through its picturesque but post-medieval market.

other ancient buildings along its three principal streets, and the area behind them is riddled with alleyways which give access to the back plots that were later developed in order to relieve the chronic housing shortage. Some thirty of Tewkesbury's ninety alleys have survived; they have a real medieval feel although they were not opened up until the end of the seventeenth century.

Heading back into the Cotswolds, we come to **Sudeley Castle**. John Leland recounts a curious anecdote which says much about the delicate position of the mighty barons in their relations to the monarch:

> Kynge Edward the fourthe bare no good will to the Lorde Sudeley, as a man suspectyd to be in hart Henry the 6. man; whereupon by complaynts he was attachid, and goinge up to London he lokyd from the hill to Sudeley, and sayde, 'Sudley castelle thou art a traytor, not I.' After he made an honest declaration, and sould his castle of Sudeley to Kynge Edward.

The implication of this cautionary tale must be that it was the possession of the powerful castle which made Lord Sudeley doubly suspect in the eyes of the King. Sudeley poses no threat any longer: its baronial frontage is patently of the nineteenth century, but it is worth inspecting the ruins of the once magnificent banqueting hall with its gorgeous array of elegant windows.

Near by are the remains of **Hailes Abbey**, a Cistercian monastery of Cotswolds limestone, displaying an uncommonly fine taste for decorative tiles and stone carving. The reason for such opulence was perhaps its royal foundation by the brother of Henry III, Richard, Earl of Cornwall in 1246. Even with its royal patronage Hailes Abbey did not prosper for long, but its fortunes were greatly revived in 1270 when Richard's son Edmund donated a few precious drops of Christ's Holy Blood which had been authenticated by the Patriarch of Jerusalem. This relic – however dubious its authenticity – was enough to spark off an enormous interest in Hailes as a new pilgrimage shrine. The flood of pilgrims' donations financed a rebuilding of the east end of the church, converting the square apse into a spectacular cluster of seven radiating chapels. Sadly, the destruction of Hailes Abbey has been severe, but some of the cloister arcading remains in place. The site museum offers some tantalising glimpses of the quality of the craftsmanship deployed by masons and tilemakers.

As the road rises up the western slopes of the Cotswolds, the car traveller catches a fleeting glimpse of an idyllic landscape that could have been taken straight from the Middle Ages. A tiny village with church and manor nestles in the crook of a wooded slope with a foreground of open fields. This same scene was also noted by John Leland in the 1530s, who described it as: ' **Stanway** village, standynge in the rotes of the hills caullyd Coteswolde. There is in Stanwey a fayre manor place and lordshipe, at the east end of the churche, a late longing to the abbay of Tweukesbyri, where he some tyme lay.' And so it all stands today, with Stanway House peeping over the east end of the churchyard. It is in such places that intervals of hundreds of years can be bridged in an instant, giving a real sense to the old cliché of timeless charm.

From here there are many possible routes back through the Cotswolds, but a serious medieval trail should take in **Chipping Campden**, another of the great wool towns and home of William Grevel, whose memorial brass in the parish church hails him poetically as 'the flower of all the wool merchants of all England'. Grevel was originally a Londoner, but he made his fortune here in Chipping Campden where he died in 1401. His mansion still stands on a prime site by the marketplace, not a brazen piece of architecture, but quietly solid and prosperous, oblivious to the passage of the years.

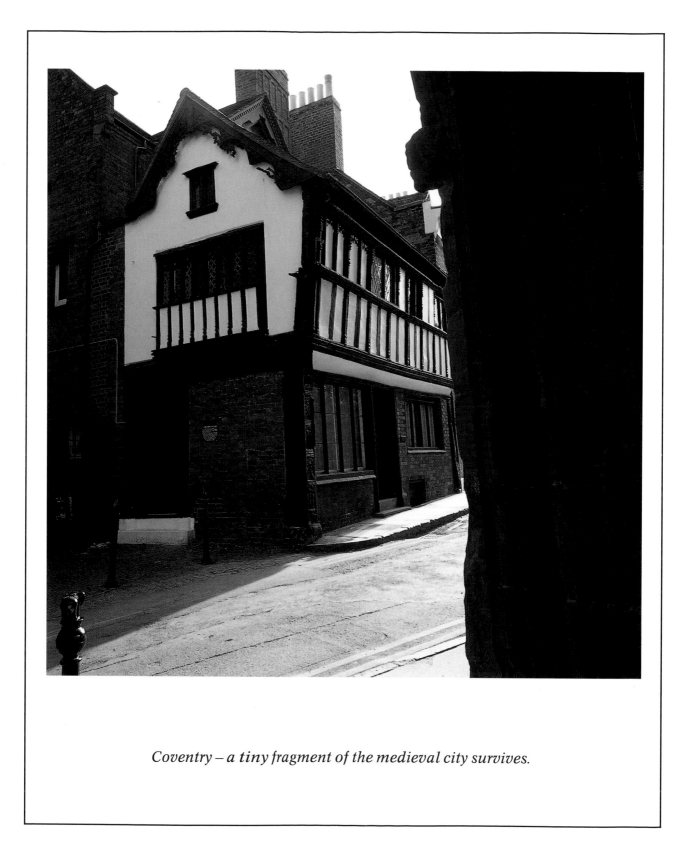

Coventry – a tiny fragment of the medieval city survives.

V. THE MIDLANDS

OVENTRY IS THE SETTING for one of the most famous and ambivalent legends of medieval England, Lady Godiva's notorious naked ride on horseback through the streets of the town. Roger of Wendover, writing in 1237 some 150 years after the event, provides the earliest version of the story. The noble lady had been persistently pleading with her husband Leofric to free the citizens of Coventry from a particularly burdensome toll until he, in evident exasperation, retorted with the bizarre reply:

> Ride naked through the length of the market, when the people are gathered together, and when thou returnest, thy petition shall be fulfilled . . . Then the countess, beloved of God, loosened her hair thus veiling her body, and then, mounting her horse and attended by two knights, she rode through the market seen of none, her white legs nevertheless appearing; and having completed her journey, returned to her husband rejoicing, and . . . obtained from him what she had asked.

The erotic element in the legend of Godiva's 'womanly pertinacity' has ensured its survival over the centuries and serves as an effective reminder of Coventry's early medieval origins; for the town first took its existence from the Benedictine monastery founded around 1050 by Leofric and Godiva not long before the Norman Conquest, although the etymology of 'convent town' is rather dubious. The illustrious pair were eventually buried in noble style in their minster church, but nothing remains of this building which has vanished along with nearly all of Coventry's medieval heritage.

Indeed, apart from the Godiva legend, Coventry – that archetype of the Midlands industrial city – might seem a strange place to go in search of medieval England. However, prior to the devastating air raid of 14–15 November 1940 the city was a veritable treasure-house of the artistic and urban achievements of the Middle Ages. Although much had already been sacrificed to the march of progress, it is essentially true that on that fateful night one of the great medieval cities of Europe was reduced to rubble and ashes. However, it is worth exploring the few survivals of what was the leading centre of the Midlands cloth trade for several centuries.

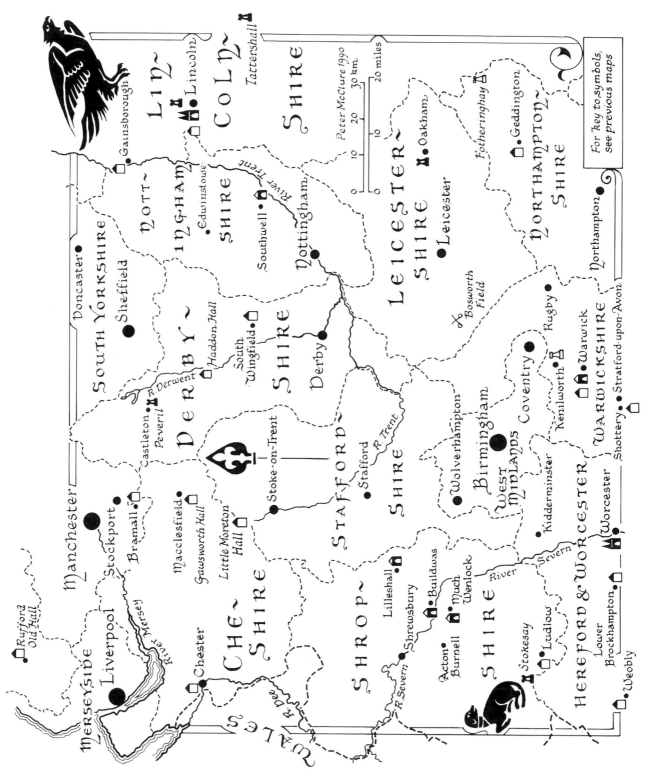

LIN~
COLN~
SHIRE

• Gainsborough

⚔ • Lincoln
Lincoln

• Tattershall

NOTT~
INGHAM~
SHIRE

• Edwinstowe

Southwell •

• Nottingham

Peter McClure 1990

30 km
20 miles

20
10
10

LEICESTER~
SHIRE

⚔ • Oakham
Oakham

• Leicester
Leicester

• Fotheringhay

• Geddington

NORTHAMPTON~
SHIRE

• Northampton

For key to symbols,
see previous maps

River Trent

• Doncaster

SOUTH YORKSHIRE

• Sheffield

DERBY~
SHIRE

• Haddon Hall

South
Wingfield •

Bosworth
Field ⚔

WARWICKSHIRE

• Rugby

• Warwick
Warwick

⚔ • Kenilworth
Kenilworth

Stratford-upon-Avon •
• Shottery

• Derby

• Castleton
Peveril

Stoke-on-Trent •

STAFFORD~
SHIRE

• Stafford

R. Trent

• Wolverhampton

Birmingham •
WEST
MIDLANDS

• Coventry

• Kidderminster

Manchester •

Stockport •

• Bramall
Bramall

• Macclesfield

Gawsworth Hall

Little Moreton
Hall

Rufford
Old Hall

Liverpool •

MERSEYSIDE

River Mersey

• Chester

CHE~
SHIRE

R. Dee

WALES

Lilleshall •

SHROP~
SHIRE

Shrewsbury •

• Buildwas
• Much
Wenlock

Acton •
Burnell

R. Severn

River Severn

• Ludlow

• Stokesay

HEREFORD & WORCESTER
SHIRE

• Worcester

Lower
Brockhampton •

• Weobly

R. Derwent

The old parish church of **St Michael**, elevated to cathedral status in 1918, remains as an empty shell, roofless and brooding, a silent witness to the past, now serving as a forecourt to the brave new Coventry Cathedral of the 1950s. Just outside the south door of St Michael's lurks an isolated relic of the old city, **St Mary's Hall**, originally built between 1340 and 1460 as the hall and chambers of the Merchant Guilds of St Mary and Holy Trinity. A few steps away at 22 Bayley Lane stands a house of about 1500 vintage, the last timber-framed structure to be found in the area. In this quiet backwater it is just possible to think of Coventry as a city of some antiquity. Another remarkable item is the great dormitory of the Carmelites or White Friars, an eleven-bay structure under a sixteenth-century roof; and in Spon Street there are a number of timber-framed houses and shops which allow a tantalising glimpse of Coventry's vanished medieval streetscapes.

Not far to the south of Coventry, the ruins of **Kenilworth Castle** do not have to contend with any modern intrusion. The protective curtain wall of red sandstone holds the castle aloof from the nearby town. Building was commenced here in the twelfth century by Geoffrey de Clinton, Treasurer to Henry I, but the castle was appropriated to the Crown by Henry II. The massive yet elegant Norman keep of 1180 is a magnificent specimen of its type. In the 1370s Kenilworth was remodelled by John of Gaunt. His Great Hall is now ruinous, although something of its former magnificence is conveyed by the stately oriel windows.

But the real fascination at Kenilworth lies in the tangible evidence it gives of that tremendous turning point in the sixteenth century when the legacy of the Middle Ages was met and modified by the new ideas of the Tudor Renaissance. This may be appreciated in the work of the last of Kenilworth's builders, Robert Dudley the Earl of Leicester and, more significantly, the favourite of Queen Elizabeth I. Robert Dudley updated the Norman keep by installing generously proportioned, square, mullioned windows; and he built a castellated gatehouse which re-introduced the round Roman arch after centuries dominated by the pointed or broken arch of the Gothic style. But his greatest innovation was an entirely new range which is still known as Leicester's Buildings, constructed with an eye to hosting his beloved Elizabeth on one of her royal progresses through England. These visitations of the Queen with her retinue of hundreds of courtiers and servants were invariably an expensive undertaking for the host and one which only the wealthiest of noblemen could contemplate with equanimity.

Elizabeth descended on Kenilworth for nineteen days during the hot July of 1575. During that brief time the Earl of Leicester disbursed on entertainment, gifts and sundry diversions almost as much as the costs incurred by Sir John Thynne for the entire building of Longleat House. From eyewitness sources we have vivid accounts of courtly dances, fireworks by moonlight, sumptuous banquets, parades of silk and jewelled costumes, dramatic performances, bear baiting, hunting parties and concerts on the lake which once formed part of the castle's defences. This was Kenilworth's Indian Summer, for when Elizabeth moved on, no

A CONVERTED KEEP. *The Norman centrepiece of Kenilworth Castle in Warwickshire was updated in the sixteenth century by Robert Dudley, Earl of Leicester. Note the Renaissance-style windows he had inserted.*

A TOMB FIT FOR A KING. *The funerary memorial of Richard Beauchamp, Earl of Warwick, in the Beauchamp Chapel of the Church of St Mary in Warwick is one of the most splendid burials in the whole of England.*

such splendour was ever to be seen again within its walls. The Leicester Buildings are now open to the skies, haunted only by memories; and the melodies of the minstrels have been replaced by the cawing of rooks who fly at will through the glassless mullioned windows.

At **Warwick** there is another fine castle in a majestic setting, but it remained in occupation as a private residence until as recently as 1978 and offers a medley of nineteenth-century apartments within a fourteenth-century curtain wall. Warwick's most glorious medieval treasure lies in the **Beauchamp Chapel** of the Church of St Mary in the centre of the town. Take a deep breath as you step into what is certainly the grandest non-royal chantry in the country. Its centrepiece is the resplendent tomb of Richard Beauchamp, Earl of Warwick. It inspired this description by John Leland in the 1530s: 'This stately pece of worke was after made by the executors of his testament, and there he is entumbid right princly, and porturyd with an image of coper and gilt, hoped over with staves of coper and gilt lyke a chariot.'

Even Leland's 'right princly' cannot prepare us for the sheer splendour of the arrangement. There lies this effigy of the Earl of Warwick upon a lofty tomb chest, clad in a gilded suit of Milanese full-plate armour. There is some doubt about the likeness of the noble countenance which gazes through raised hands held slightly apart, frozen in a gesture of adoration of the Virgin, whose statue gazes down from above. The chariot represented by the staves is a stylised version of a medieval hearse, probably a reference to that which brought the body back from Rouen where Richard Beauchamp died in 1439 as Lieutenant of France. For this is none other than the notorious Earl of Warwick who signed the death warrant of Joan of Arc, and thereby condemned her to death by burning at the stake. There are many who would agree that such a man was sorely in need of all the masses sung in his chantry chapel in order to speed the passage of his soul through purgatory. That other Earl of Warwick, 'The Kingmaker', appears as one of the gilt figures of the weepers which adorn the sides of the tomb.

About 150 years after the decease of Richard Beauchamp it was the turn of Robert Dudley, Earl of Leicester, to be interred in the Beauchamp Chapel in 1588. The generous host, erstwhile favourite and reputed lover of Elizabeth I, is shown in effigy alongside his wife in an image of conjugal fidelity which hardly corresponds to the reality of the situation. Some might consider the Dudleys to be interlopers in the Beauchamp Chapel, but they do add to the general effect. Robert Dudley left another mark on the town of Warwick in the attractive group of half-timbered buildings lying hard by the west gate. Founded in 1571, the **Leycester Hospital** took over the premises of the combined Guilds of Holy Trinity and St George; and some older medieval structures are to be found within. It now serves as a home for retired soldiers.

Such is the aura that Shakespeare's fame has left hanging over the neighbouring town of **Stratford-upon-Avon** that the whole place still bathes in the gentle afterglow of the Elizabethan era. It is not easy to penetrate the quaintness of the half-timbered heritage, much of it none too ancient, and to take stock of the authentic medieval content. The last description of pre-Shakespearian Stratford comes from the quill of John Leland, who passed through at least a quarter of a century before the birth of the playwright in 1564. Leland noted the **Gild Chapel** dedicated to the Holy Trinity, its adjoining 'gramar-schole' and 'an almose-house of 10. pore folke', all of which have survived to create one of the best groupings of medieval buildings to be seen. Here one can savour the variety of a streetscape where the pointed gables of wooden houses are punctuated by bolder structures of stone. The Gild Chapel retains some vestiges of a vast mural painting above the chancel arch depicting that ever popular medieval subject, 'The Dance of Death'. Leland

The Leycester Hospital in Warwick is still occupied.

also informs us that 'The bysshope of Worcester is lorde of the towne'. In fact, Stratford-upon-Avon was the creation of a much earlier Bishop of Worcester who began the transformation of a sleepy farming hamlet in the twelfth century. It was but one of many deliberate acts of town creation at the time, and one which has prospered and endured.

Although he belongs to the Tudor period, let us return to Shakespeare for a moment, for it should be noted that young William attended the grammar school in Stratford, and the medieval classroom where he first had to grapple with the vagaries of Latin is still in service, though now but a tiny element of a much larger establishment, the King's School. Shakespeare would have been familiar also with the **Church of the Holy Trinity** on the banks of the Avon, a short distance from the town's commercial centre, which is noted for its superb east window in the Perpendicular style and its finely carved misericords. Architectural pundits tend to be dismissive about the value of those famous Shakespearian shrines, the Birth Place and the New Place, but these buildings, albeit much restored, are atmospheric examples of late medieval and Tudor domestic comfort. The same applies to **Anne Hathaway's Cottage** at Shottery, about a mile from the centre of Stratford. Part of this

TWO FACES OF MEDIEVAL STRATFORD. *Forget Shakespeare for a moment, and admire an original streetscape of the Middle Ages by the Gild Chapel* (left). *However, it is thanks to the fame of the bard that Anne Hathaway's cottage at Shottery* (above) *has been restored.*

building was destroyed by fire a few years ago and was subsequently reconstructed from beams removed from other redundant houses of similar antiquity. The rebuilt cottage has now mellowed and sits happily enough behind its informal period garden, defying anyone to challenge its authenticity.

Further west, on the banks of the Severn, there rises the noble shape of **Worcester Cathedral**. Its foundation goes back to 1084, just after the Conquest, but nothing remains of the work inaugurated by the Anglo-Saxon Bishop Wulfstan but the exquisite crypt. The most illustrious occupant of the cathedral is King John, whose effigy and mortal remains repose in the choir. Remembered chiefly as the treacherous brother of the chivalrous Richard Lionheart, and as the reluctant signatory of the Magna Carta in 1215, King John has little hope of shrugging off his ignoble image. However, his crowned likeness as an effigy is nothing less than regal, although the blackish Purbeck marble will continue to suggest a sombre and sinister side to his character. King John died ingloriously on 18 October 1216 in Newark Castle, having sustained a debilitating bout of dysentery, but his body was brought to Worcester at his own request. Windsor and Westminster were not yet the automatic choice of last resting place for the kings and queens of England.

A more humble medieval relic awaits further to the west in the village of **Lower Brockhampton** where an early fifteenth-century moated manor house presents the very picture of half-timbered perfection. The house is typical of late medieval yeoman domesticity and still meets all the requirements of a comfortable home, in contrast to the dank, dark and chilly vaults of the grander castles of stone. The nearby village of **Weobley** gives an exceptionally strong impression of the overall scale and harmony of large groups of basic medieval housing. Many of the houses are of cruck construction, where the frame is provided by two mighty beams rising directly from the ground to support the ridge pole. Where the beams have not been plastered over, this is an architecture of dramatic structural transparency.

Here in the counties along the Welsh border, the imprint of the Middle Ages has been less modified by the process of rebuilding than elsewhere in England. At **Ludlow** the outline of the medieval town may still be recognised with its castle, huddled streets and majestic church tower of St Lawrence dominating the scene. The castle has its entry in the annals of English history as the place where Prince Arthur died in 1502, leaving the path to the throne open to his younger brother, the future Henry VIII. In Ludlow we may well speculate how the course of events might have been changed had Arthur survived to be king: whether the destruction of the Dissolution would have been averted and the progress of the Reformation altered. Would he have been crowned Arthur I or II? For the prince was named by his father Henry VII as a way of claiming some form of descent from the legendary King Arthur of the Celts.

To the north of Ludlow, the fortified manor of **Stokesay Castle** presents a fairytale image of medieval picturesque. The assemblage of stone walls is rendered delightful and endearing by the timber-framed superstructure added in the fifteenth century. Doubtless the proximity

Lower Brockhampton, quintessence of half-timbered yeoman England.

of Ludlow Castle had brought a degree of security to the region, enough to permit the wealthy wool merchant Lawrence Ludlow in about the year 1280 to set himself up in such quasi-baronial state so close to the territory of the fierce warriors of Wales. The elegant Gothic windows of his Great Hall would have been vulnerable to any assault. The Jacobean gatehouse, built in 1620, is more symbolic and decorative than functional in any real sense. An essential part of the medieval feel of Stokesay Castle lies in its intimate proximity to the church, underlining the two poles of rural life, the lord of the manor and the parish priest. Just a few miles away at **Acton Burnell** lie the ruins of another fortified manor, also going back to the closing decades of the thirteenth century; but this was once a more imposing tower house, reflecting the status of its owner Bishop Burnell of Wells.

Within the orbit of Shrewsbury are scattered the remains of several once important monastic houses. **Wenlock Priory** was a Cluniac foundation, still distinguished by the quality of its blank interlaced arcading. The church of **Buildwas Abbey** is almost intact but for its roof and provides a textbook example of early Cistercian austerity. **Lilleshall Abbey** and **Haughmond Abbey** belonged to the Augustinians; the latter retains some of the figurative sculptures which decorated the church and which would have been shunned as excessive ostentation by the Cistercian brethren at Buildwas.

The road north leads to **Chester** which occupies the site of Roman Deva; and the

BLACK AND WHITE. *The stark contrast of wood and plaster in fanciful decorative devices may be seen all over the north-west of England. Gawsworth Hall in Cheshire is a noted example of the genre.*

A LONG GALLERY FOR RAINY DAYS. *In response to the new architectural trends of the sixteenth century, a long gallery was created at Little Moreton Hall which runs the entire length of the west wing's upper floor. A Renaissance flourish to a medieval house.*

The city walls of Chester.

medieval walls stand partly on the foundations of those built soon after AD 79 around the legionary fortress. Chester's walls have been restored on many occasions, so that much of the visible fabric is modern rather than medieval, but they feel authentic enough and their 2½ miles represent England's sole surviving complete circuit around a town. Walking the walls in Chester is still an exciting experience. It takes no great effort of the imagination to conjure up that potent polarity of urban life *intra muros* and rural life *extra muros* with originally nothing suburban in between to blur the effect. On the one side there were rolling fields, pockets of woodland and scattered hamlets; on the other lay the medieval labyrinth with shops and houses amidst noble churches and the cathedral in an enclave of elegant urbanity.

The centre of Chester is renowned for the 'Rows', a cunning arrangement of galleries which allows shops to operate at two levels. The upper floor consists of a covered arcade with wooden balustrades, to which there is access via a number of steep and narrow staircases. The charm of this contrivance is so captivating that it takes a while to realise that most of Chester's apparently medieval or Tudor buildings, despite their eye-dazzling 'magpie' façades, are rather too large and regular to be authentic. In fact, the vast majority are late Victorian and indicate the highwater mark of the Tudor Revival which swept the board of domestic architecture in England towards the end of the nineteenth century. Those with a taste for the real thing should investigate some of the early medieval cellars of Chester, dating back to the thirteenth century.

The difference between Victorian fake half-timbering, as may be experienced in Chester, and the genuine article can be profitably observed at **Little Moreton Hall** in Cheshire. This is undoubtedly one of the loveliest houses of any category in the whole of England. Its building history straddles the fifteenth and sixteenth centuries, showing how Tudor fashions were introduced such as the two great bow windows which push forward into the courtyard, one literally grafted on to the traditional Great Hall and drawing in a flood of light. Most novel of all was the construction of the south wing by John Moreton in the 1570s. This is a much less solid structure than the medieval part of the house; and one can imagine that older and wiser tongues wagged about the shoddy quality of the new work, especially when at the last moment it was decided to add a 68-foot Long Gallery running the full length of the block. That the structure was not designed to withstand the additional weight may be readily appreciated. The twisted and buckled planks and beams give one the feeling of walking the deck of a wooden galleon riding a choppy sea. A striking design feature is the continuous row of windows; and an indication that the Long Gallery was used for games and exercise was provided by the discovery of a seventeenth-century tennis ball behind the wainscotting.

The exterior of Little Moreton Hall, with its distinctive cloverleaf decoration reflects a fashion that was particularly in vogue in Cheshire and Lancashire. **Gawsworth Hall** near Macclesfield and **Bramall Hall** on the outskirts of Stockport show the same delight in bold monochromatic effects. The oldest parts of Bramall Hall go back to 1375, but the general effect of the building today is resolutely Tudor. **Rufford Old Hall** in Lancashire, although quite a detour from this present journey, is a much more authentic expression of the Middle Ages. The wonderful fifteenth-century hall has an ornate hammerbeam roof and a handsomely carved screen which gave the noble master of the house something more pleasant to contemplate than the kitchens beyond.

From the lush pastures of Cheshire there is a dramatic change of scenery as the way heads east up into the bleaker landscapes of the Peak District. On a triangular spur of rock looming high above the Derbyshire village of Castleton squats the ancient hulk of **Peveril Castle**. The dominant feature of the remains is the sturdy stone keep built by Henry II, but the curtain wall on the more exposed north flank dates back to the original castle put up soon after the Conquest, indeed early enough to be mentioned in Domesday Book in 1086. Stone was chosen from the outset for this remote fortification, for there was no wooden predecessor on the site, as was the usual practice for the first generation of Norman castles in England. Peveril's strategic purpose seems to have been the defence of the rich lead mines in the area. Or was it also to enforce discipline on the miners, whose lives must have been a grim penal sentence of hard labour from which only disability or death procured a release?

Haddon Hall, also in Derbyshire, evokes pleasanter images of life much nearer the top of medieval society. Its period character has been retained by successive Dukes of Rutland right into the twentieth century. Its private chapel has conserved some remarkable murals, notably a moving portrayal of St Christopher bearing the Infant Christ on his shoulder through the turbulent waters of a river in flood. The courtyard of Haddon Hall is a wonderful spatial composition which reveals itself gradually to visitors as they make their way through the gatehouse and up a slope and a bent flight of stairs. This is still a living house, by contrast to **South Wingfield Manor House**, also in Derbyshire, which has been lying abandoned for centuries. This was built by an Agincourt veteran Ralph, Lord Cromwell, who served as Constable of Nottingham Castle, Warden of Sherwood Forest and finally as the Chancellor of England. The magnificence of the building reflects the fruits of success, symbolised by the emblem of the bulging money bag carved over the inner entrance

A COURTYARD BECKONS. *The entrancing courtyard of Haddon Hall in Derbyshire opens up a thrilling vista of the ancient residence. An angled flight of steps creates an unexpected perspective.*

THE LORD TREASURER AT HOME. *South Wingfield Manor in Derbyshire was built in the 1440s by Ralph, Lord Cromwell, Chancellor of England. His emblem of double money bags is carved over the inner entrance.*

The Chapter House, Southwell Minster.

as an obvious reference to his office of state. This proud status symbol is also to be seen at Tattershall Castle in Lincolnshire, another imposing residence of Lord Cromwell, commensurate with the importance of the man who held the Treasurership of the nation from 1433 and 1443.

After inspecting so many abodes of greater and lesser magnates, it comes as a complete change to plunge once more into the often mysterious world of the medieval church. **Southwell Minster** in Nottinghamshire conceals within its muscular Norman shell one of the most delicate and elegant expressions of Gothic to be found anywhere in England. The **Chapter House**, added in the thirteenth century, has taken as its theme the artistic celebration in stone of the trees of the forest. Commenced in 1290, this was the final phase of Southwell Minster; it is reached from the choir via a passage and vestibule which give little hint of the spectacle awaiting in the wondrous octagonal chamber. There is an overwhelming flood of naturalistic stone carving which brings to life a profusion of woodland leaves: maple, oak, hawthorn, ranunculus, vine and ivy hang from the masonry as if taken directly from the forest. This covering of exquisite foliage hangs delicately over every available space on finials and crockets, corbels and capitals. Birds, beasts and even human heads peek out unexpectedly from this riot of botanic specimens, captured in stone. The pagan-inspired Green Man, a medieval tree spirit and a symbol of fertility in the folk culture of the day, appears here in his many separate guises, fully in his element. The carving contains no direct references to Christian teaching: it's as if a society still imbued with pagan memories and inspired by the natural world has heaped into the shrine of its new religion all its older hopes, fears and beliefs, in the uncomplicated trust that the one would not contradict the essential truth of the other.

Just how important it was to incorporate the most significant elements of everyday life in religious buildings may also be seen in the exterior decoration of Southwell's Chapter House which appears to celebrate the animals of the farm with carved heads of bull, boar, ram and fish. Although the exact meaning of such medieval imagery remains elusive, these symbolic carvings require in a way no explanation at all. In a sense, it is enough for us to stand and stare for a while, and simply to become familiar with these pictorial memories of the medieval mind. Emerging once more into the twentieth century, with its dearth of spiritual imagery, we are suddenly aware of the fact that our modern world is frighteningly empty of any such potent cultural equivalent to the sculptural fantasies of the Middle Ages.

From the stylised forest of Southwell Chapter House it is but a short distance to a remnant of the real thing in **Sherwood Forest**. What remains would not conceal for long a band of outlaws such as the 'Merrie Men' of the medieval folk hero Robin Hood. Leaving aside the serious claims of Barnsdale in West Yorkshire to be the authentic lair of Robin Hood, the ancient oaks of Sherwood near Edwinstowe do provide a valid and fascinating link with the Middle Ages. The oldest tree, the **Major Oak**, goes back more than 500 years and still stands defiantly like a retired colossus or an invalided leviathan, for its mighty branches are now propped up by the felled trunks of much younger trees. So vulnerable is this veteran of the forest that it has been fenced off to prevent the weight of human visitors compressing the earth around its roots. Near by, in an area called Birkland, there are numerous gnarled trunks of dead oak, skeletons of the forest, nature's equivalent to the ruined masonry of abbeys and castles, relics of a bygone age. The appeal of the Robin Hood legend and its escapist dream of a free life in the Greenwood is even more potent today than during the Middle Ages, when vast areas of native woodland still extended over broad swathes of England and a squirrel could travel for miles without touching the ground.

However much fun it may seem to us, Robin Hood's woodland exile certainly lacked the creature comforts provided by a well-run household. **Gainsborough Old Hall** in Lincolnshire gives a better idea than most of the conviviality of a large medieval establishment, albeit from the fifteenth century. The present manor house was almost entirely rebuilt shortly before the visit of Richard III, who came to stay as a guest of Sir Thomas Burgh in 1483. The main fascination at Gainsborough is the generously proportioned kitchen with its two gaping fireplaces, each capable of accommodating an entire roast ox on a spit. In three corners of the kitchen there are small storerooms which would have been supervised by trustworthy stewards who kept a strict control over the amount of food issued to the cook. Above these larders there was access via a trapdoor to a small upper chamber which served as sleeping quarters, so that the kitchen was effectively inhabited round the clock. In winter it must have been a snug place to sleep, close to the warm chimney, but rather less pleasant on a hot summer's night. Whatever the season, it is unlikely that the kitchen staff ever managed to rid themselves of the smoke and greasy smells of roast meat and fowl.

Heading south through the flat cornfields of Lincolnshire there open up memorable views of **Lincoln Cathedral** perched on its high limestone plateau. When seen at a great distance, a fuller appreciation of the communicational power of the cathedral imposes itself. At close quarters we lose ourselves in the architectural details and are overawed by the soaring vaults

INSIDE LINCOLN CATHEDRAL. *A great church is more than the sum of its parts; but one of the delights of a cathedral is the discovery of its various features such as Lincoln's Chapter House* (above) *and the Decorated Gothic tracery of the cloister* (right).

Medieval streetscape in Lincoln's Michaelgate.

and towers, but when we first catch sight of a great cathedral such as Lincoln many miles before reaching the city itself, so it becomes obvious that it was designed to be admired also as a silhouette on the horizon, radiating a visual reminder of the Christian faith over as large an area as possible, like a spiritual beacon planted for maximum effect. Within Lincoln's Upper City, relatively untouched by development, the towers of the cathedral play a game of hide-and-seek, at one moment picturesquely framed as one stands looking up **Michaelgate**, and then hidden from view, only to make a dramatic reappearance over **Exchecquergate**. The best prospect of all is the grandstand view from the ramparts of **Lincoln Castle**.

The See of Lincoln once extended from Humberside to the Thames Valley and was the largest in England. The Bishop's Seat was transferred to Lincoln from Dorchester in Oxfordshire in 1072; and the great stature of the cathedral must be seen in this context. Its noblest benefactor, both in his own lifetime and posthumously through contributions at his shrine, was Bishop Hugh, later canonised as St Hugh of Avalon. After the earthquake of 1185 this Carthusian monk from France supervised the rebuilding of Lincoln Cathedral in the revolutionary Gothic style. Some Norman work remains in the west front where biblical scenes such as Noah's Ark and Adam and Eve compete with motifs of clearly pagan Norse mythology. Bishop Hugh's shrine in the Angel Choir is surveyed by the popular Lincoln Imp, another enigmatic piece of medieval masonry. Bishop Hugh's nearby palace has fallen into ruins but the vaulted undercroft is a powerful sight. Another Bishop of Lincoln, Hugh of Wells, was present at the sealing of Magna Carta in 1215, perhaps because Runnymede lay just within his diocese. His copy of the Magna Carta, one of only four originals, has been kept in Lincoln ever since and may now be seen in the City and County Museum, a fittingly medieval shrine since this building originally served as the chapel and undercroft of the

Franciscan Friary.

Lincoln possesses some rare relics of early medieval housing in the shape of several neat stone dwellings dating back to the twelfth century. Such substantial homes were usually the residences of Jewish moneylenders, men of considerable wealth and able to afford something more durable than the half-timbering and wattle and daub that was the run of the mill for urban housing at the time. The most famous is called, not surprisingly, the **Jew's House**; next door in The Strait is another called **Jew's Court**, both dating to the 1170s. A bit higher up, at the bottom of Steep Hill, stands a third example of the same period, which was once referred to as Aaron's House; but since it has been proved that the Aaron in question lived elsewhere in Lincoln, it has been renamed simply the **Norman House**. Aaron of Lincoln was rumoured to be the richest and most influential moneylender of his day, always involved in delicate and lucrative transactions with the Crown, but the same is also claimed for his main rival Jacob of Canterbury.

Before heading south it is of great historical fascination to travel east to the ruins of **Bolingbroke Castle**; modest though they are, these overgrown ramparts are all that stands of the castle built between 1220–30 by the Earl of Lincoln which was the birthplace of Henry Bolingbroke who took the crown from Richard II in 1399 to become Henry IV. It is hard to visualise the scene as the future founder of the House of Lancaster entered the world over 600 years ago. The castle ruins are now grazed by sheep which help keep the rampant meadow under control, but they are still the official property of the Duchy of Lancaster.

In a much better state of preservation, the proud keep of **Tattershall Castle** looms large above the Lincolnshire countryside. This late medieval fantasy was built by the same Ralph, Lord Cromwell whom we encountered at South Wingfield in Derbyshire. The idea of the seigneurial tower with its decorative machicolation is reckoned to be a borrowing from France, but the choice of material, red bricks made at the site, reflects the growing fashion in England for these humble blocks of baked earth which have been the mainstay of English architecture ever since. The construction of Tattershall Castle proceeded from 1432 to 1448 and was roughly contemporaneous with Eton College. Although the attempt at external display of decorative brickwork does not bear comparison with Eton, Tattershall is impressive on account of the versatile use of brick throughout, even to reproduce the effect of Gothic ribbed vaulting, for which the natural medium is stone. The most endearing feature of the castle, reached after climbing past three upper floors of noble chambers where the emblem of the moneypurse adorns the chimneypieces, is an enchanting roof terrace framed by a brick arcade, rather like a cloistered quadrangle in the sky. Here one can imagine Lord Cromwell's noble household promenading in their finery and enjoying a view that might have extended as far as Lincoln on a clear day. This must have been a wonderful place to take the air, soaring high over the countryside, and a magical playground for children away from the gloomy confinement of their brick-vaulted quarters. But the children who played here were not those of the creator of the Great Tower, for Ralph, Lord

THE HEALTH OF OUR SOULS. *This was the motivation behind the collegiate church founded by the master of Tattershall Castle, Lincolnshire* (above) *as of the establishment at Fotheringhay, Northamptonshire* (left) *of this imposing shrine of the House of York.*

Cromwell, died without issue, and he bequeathed much of his estate towards the construction of a collegiate church next to the castle where prayers and masses could be offered for the salvation of his soul. The church, albeit without its stained glass, still provides an effective counterpoint to the castle, which might well have been reduced to a ruinous pile by now but for the timely intervention of Lord Curzon in 1911. He purchased and restored Tattershall Castle, even retrieving and reinstating the stone chimneypieces which had been sold as baronial fixtures to collectors in America.

Oakham Castle in Leicestershire looks unimposing from the outside. All that remains of the Norman castle is the Great Hall, a free-standing structure which may at first glance be taken for a tithe barn. However, the interior is renowned for the quality of its stone carving, and it ranks as the earliest aisled hall of stone in Britain still intact. Dating back to the 1180s, it conveys more powerfully than elsewhere the domestic refinement of the Norman period. Precise parallels to the carving at Canterbury Cathedral show beyond doubt that this was the product of masons who had worked under the direction of the inspirational William of Sens. Try to ignore the absurd collection of oversized horseshoes donated by visiting aristocrats which cover the walls and admire the finely incised capitals and sculptures of a host of medieval characters, especially the musicians. By torch or candlelight these carved figures would have acquired a life of their own and provided a pleasing sight to the lord and his retinue at dinner.

At the Northamptonshire village of **Fotheringhay** there is an eery feeling of an absence rather than a presence, for this was the scene of great and tragic events in the history of the monarchy, but there is little left to tell the tale. Fotheringhay Castle is marked on the map, just beyond the attractive stone bridge, though there is nothing to be seen now but some grass-covered mounds in a field grazed by cattle from the nearby farm. It takes some effort to believe that it was here that the future Richard III was born in 1452, and here that the romantic figure of Mary Queen of Scots was confined and finally executed in 1587, convicted on the evidence of her own letters intercepted by a local brewer who was loyal to Elizabeth I. But the absence of Fotheringhay Castle is total and complete: it's as if the travelling circus of royalty simply folded its tents in the night and vanished before dawn.

Yet there is one solid testimonial to Fotheringhay's royal associations. The collegiate church built by Richard, Duke of York, in the 1430s, albeit bereft of its choir, raises its octagonal belfry atop its square tower in a cathedral-like gesture of majesty. The church has been described as a shrine of the House of York, and its symbolic value was evidently not lost on Elizabeth I. She ordered the decayed tombs of Richard III's parents to be rebuilt in the nave as a token of political reconciliation perhaps, for it was her ancestor Henry Tudor in 1485 who defeated Richard III at Bosworth Field and brought the ambitions of the House of York to an end.

But there is another moving episode of royal history to evoke in Northamptonshire before proceeding to Bosworth Field in Leicestershire. In the village of **Geddington** there stands a richly decorated three-sided monument. This is one of several which were erected by Edward I to commemorate the funeral cortège of his wife, Eleanor of Castile which made its painful way from Lincoln to London during the December of 1290. Only two other Eleanor Crosses survive, at Hardingstone on the southern outskirts of Northampton and at Waltham Cross near London. These symbols of Edward's personal grief serve also as a warning that historical personalities are usually more complex than their reputations. The English king, who has been nicknamed 'The Hammer of the Scots', was also a man of deep emotional resonance, as witnessed by his words for Eleanor: 'We always

Eleanor Cross, Geddington, Northamptonshire.

loved her for as long as she lived. We will not cease to love her now that she is dead.'

And so to **Bosworth Field**, where in 1485 the crown of England was lost and won; and the colourful Tudor dynasty was inaugurated in the person of Henry VII. As for the death of Richard III, we have Shakespeare's words, 'A horse! A horse! My kingdom for a horse!' to remind us that the hapless king was on foot when he was eventually hacked down. The exact spot is marked by a memorial stone on an obscure piece of ground which is now wedged between a canal and a disused railway. Such inauspicious surroundings suggest that there is in the long run nothing glorious in the death of kings, but Bosworth Field concerns more than the slaying of Richard III for it concluded that long and bloody chapter of medieval England, known almost poetically as the War of the Roses.

The Cistercian ruins at Roche Abbey, Yorkshire.

VI. YORKSHIRE

THE BLEACHED BONES of the great abbeys of Yorkshire still provide the most enduring images of the county. The 'bare ruin'd choirs where late the sweet birds sang' in such splendid churches as Fountains, Rievaulx and Whitby are still alive in the post-industrial era. So powerful is their serene presence, whether under a sky of blue or brooding grey, that the impression is easily given that Yorkshire was the spiritual fountainhead for the monastic ideal of the entire nation. In fact, the county's first wave of founding fervour in the seventh century was of Northumbrian inspiration, led by saints such as Hilda, Cedd and Wilfrid; and its second, after a pagan Viking interlude, came in the wake of the Norman Conquest some time after the south of England had already been liberally sprinkled with abbeys and priories. The Benedictines, those pioneers of monasticism in the Norman mould, established only three houses in Yorkshire, at Selby, Whitby and York. However, the county was to provide ideal and virgin territory for the reformed orders from the twelfth century onwards. Above all, it was the Cistercians or 'white monks', whose quest for austerity, remoteness and self-sufficiency at the outer edges of human society drew them to the wild moors and dales of Yorkshire. Here, on the roof of England nature was still unsubdued and the sky, seeming both wider and closer, conveyed a more direct and elemental experience of God. Other orders also came north to build great monasteries, but the Cistercians really made the land their own.

Approaching through the south, there is at **Roche Abbey** a delightful overture to the grand Cistercian symphony awaiting further to the north. Although modest in the extent of its upstanding remains, Roche shows all the essentials of the typical Cistercian layout. The groundplan comprises a large range of quarters for the lay brethren who provided the sweated labour for what was typically a thriving agricultural business. The monastic buildings straddle a pretty stream, for fresh water was a vital element for sanitation as well as for consumption. Here the stream was channelled to run directly beneath the euphemistically named 'reredorter' or toilet block. But the surrounding landscape at Roche owes its present appearance not to the Cistercians but to the romantic vision of Capability Brown in the eighteenth century, when the taste for 'mournfull ruines' became extremely fashionable.

A few miles away to the north **Conisbrough Castle** shows the architectural sophistication

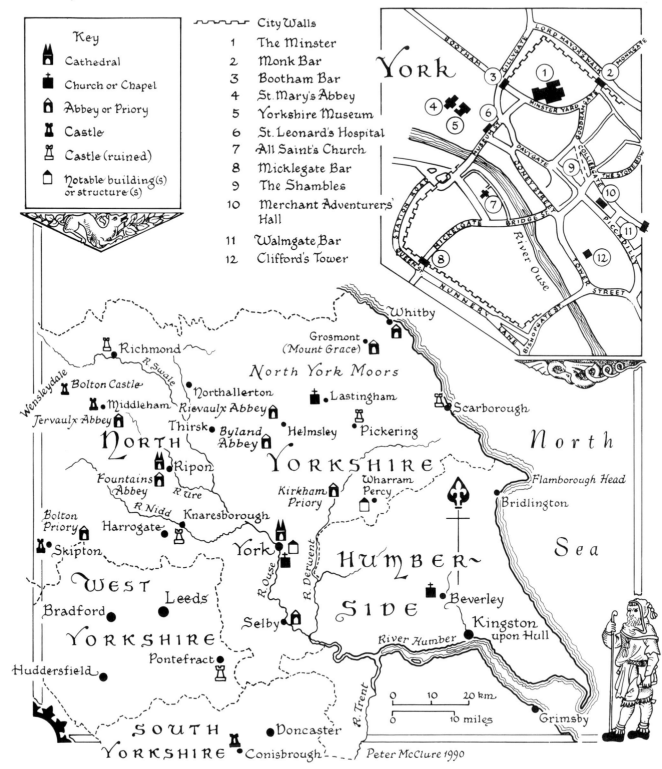

Key

- Cathedral
- Church or Chapel
- Abbey or Priory
- Castle
- Castle (ruined)
- Notable building(s) or structure(s)

City Walls
1   The Minster
2   Monk Bar
3   Bootham Bar
4   St. Mary's Abbey
5   Yorkshire Museum
6   St. Leonard's Hospital
7   All Saint's Church
8   Micklegate Bar
9   The Shambles
10   Merchant Adventurers' Hall
11   Walmgate Bar
12   Clifford's Tower

York

BOOTHAM   GILLYGATE   LORD MAYOR'S WALK   MONKGATE
3   1   2
MINSTER YARD
4
6   GOODRAMGATE
5   DEANGATE
MUSEUM ST   THE STONEBOW
9   COLLIERGATE
10
STATION ROAD   MONEY BRIER   BRIDGE ST   PICCADILLY
7   11
NICKLEGATE
8   12
QUEEN ST   River Ouse
NUNNERY LANE   BISHOPGATE ST   TOWER STREET

Whitby
Grosmont
(Mount Grace)
Richmond
R. Swale
North York Moors
Wensleydale   Bolton Castle
Northallerton   Lastingham
Middleham   Rievaulx Abbey   Scarborough
Jervaulx Abbey   Thirsk   Helmsley   Pickering
Byland   NORTH
Abbey
Ripon   YORKSHIRE   North
Fountains
Abbey   R. Ure   Kirkham   Wharram
Priory   Percy   Flamborough Head
Bolton   R. Nidd   Knaresborough   Bridlington
Priory   Harrogate
Skipton   HUMBER-   Sea
WEST   York   SIDE
Leeds   Beverley
Bradford   R. Ouse   R. Derwent
YORKSHIRE   Selby   Kingston
upon Hull
Huddersfield   River Humber
Pontefract   R. Trent
0   10   20 km
SOUTH   Doncaster
YORKSHIRE   Conisbrough   0   10 miles   Grimsby
Peter McClure 1990

of the late twelfth century in the castellar domain. The manor of Conisbrough belonged to the royal estate of Harold, the last Saxon King of England. It became part of the rich spoil granted by William the Conqueror to reward one of his chief barons, William de Warrenne. The finest feature at Conisbrough is the noble keep, built between 1180 and 1190 by Hameline Plantagenet, a half-brother of Henry II. It has come through the ages remarkably intact, partly on account of its non-combatant role during the Civil War of the seventeenth century. Although the floors of the central chambers of the keep are now missing, the truly royal quality of the work is still much in evidence. As at Orford in Suffolk, it is a never-failing source of amazement just how much has been fitted into the thick stone walls. The highlight is a small but enchanting chapel with carved roof bosses and dogtooth decoration on its vaulting; it is cunningly accommodated within one of the protruding buttresses. Everywhere, it is the sheer quality of the masonry that impresses. Stone stairways curve gracefully upwards, following the line of the building. Conisbrough was one of the very first circular keeps in England and still ranks among the very best.

The way north leads via **Pontefract**, where the ruins of the castle in a public park are not impressive on their own account, but as the place where the deposed Richard II was almost certainly murdered by his ambitious successor Henry IV. Then, veering towards the north-east, we come to **Selby**, one of the three Benedictine houses in Yorkshire. The abbey church survived the Dissolution of the 1530s only to fall victim to a serious fire in 1906. The church has been subsequently restored and is still in parochial use.

Beverley Minster is another great survivor and as wondrous a piece of architecture as any cathedral. Its fascination is heightened by a wealth of stone carvings inside which amount to the most comprehensive collection of musical instruments from the Middle Ages. We are confronted here with a veritable orchestra in stone of medieval musicians playing some seventy different instruments of the period. Viols, tambourines, bagpipes, cymbals, double horns, harps, trumpets, guitars, tabors and zithers are all in action, together with earthy portrayals of their long-forgotten players. However, all is eerily silent, as if the voices of these instruments had been silenced and frozen in stone by some magic spell. Yet so realistic are the carvings that it seems that Beverley Minster might at any moment burst back into life to the sounds of an uproarious concert that has been held in suspense for more than six centuries. The musical theme makes an encore in the choir where the humorous carver of the wooden misericords has portrayed subjects such as a monkey playing the bagpipes and a pig plucking a harp.

Music has also been represented in the intricate stone canopy of the Percy Tomb in Beverley Minster. This has been acclaimed as one of the finest examples of fourteenth-century stone carving in the Decorated style. Quite surprisingly for such an elaborate memorial, it is not known for sure who is commemorated here, but the favourite candidate is Lady Eleanor of the Percy lineage, that great family which, along with their rivals the Nevilles, has left its traces all over the northern counties. In fact, the history of the North of

ARTISTRY IN STONE. *Masons were the master craftsmen of the Middle Ages. They functioned both as architects and engineers at Conisbrough Castle* (above) *and as sculptors with such refined works as this horn player at Beverley Minster* (right).

England in the Middle Ages could largely be written from the annals of these warring, dynastic families.

By contrast, the remains of the rustic past are much less obvious to the eye than the monuments of the great and mighty. Countless farming hamlets disappeared from the map of medieval England, almost without leaving a trace on the ground. More than three thousand sites of deserted villages have now been identified in England alone, so the phenomenon is fairly common all over the country. But **Wharram Percy** has become the most famous of all, largely thanks to the efforts of the Medieval Village Research Group which has painstakingly pieced together the evolution of the place from Neolithic farm to medieval manor. Today, only the village church remains as a visible structure above ground, for it continued to be used and maintained by the villagers of Thixendale nearby until as recently as 1870. The actual peasant houses and even the larger 'manor' may be seen only as bumpy outlines in the grass. The most telling feature is the reconstructed medieval fishpond. It may be bizarre to view a pond as an archaeological monument, but this is indeed the case, for there has been a man-made pond here since Saxon times, providing generations of local folk with fish for the dinner table, a humble but effective arrangement.

At the height of its fortunes in the fourteenth century Wharram Percy was home to some 150 souls spread over thirty households. But soil exhaustion resulting from overcultivation was already taking its toll by 1323 when some two thirds of the fields were overgrown and the cornmills derelict. Then came the Black Death in 1348–9. By the middle of the fifteenth century there remained only some sixteen houses in occupation, and by around 1500 the last of them had been abandoned. Thereafter, sheep grazed the ruins of Wharram Percy, as indeed they still do, albeit at the discretion of the archaeologists.

Thanks to the almost indecent scientific investigation of the site, more is known about the domestic habits of Wharram Percy's medieval inhabitants than of anywhere else in Britain. Nevertheless, the village retains its aura of mysterious fascination. It is a longish walk from the nearest road and, with its layout increasingly mapped and exposed, it is possible in the imagination to repopulate the settlement. And so Wharram Percy lives on, albeit bereft of inhabitants, like some landlocked *Marie Celeste* sailing through the centuries as a time-capsule of the Middle Ages. It is strange to reflect that Wharram Percy has achieved infinitely more fame as an archaeological site than it ever possessed in reality as an obscure hamlet with living inhabitants.

We are back with more tangible remains at **Kirkham Priory** on the River Derwent. The gatehouse bears a splendid array of heraldic devices of the de Roos lords of Helmsley, but it was an earlier lord of that castle, Walter Espec, who founded the Augustinian priory here in the 1120s. Walter Espec later favoured the Cistercians and endowed their new abbey at Rievaulx in 1131. However, his attempts to convert Kirkham from the Augustinian to the Cistercian Rule appear to have foundered. A picturesque Norman doorway, which once led from the cloister to the refectory, now frames a pastoral scene of fat sheep grazing a lush, grassy hillside, a juxtaposition that would have appealed immensely to the Cistercians, those industrious sheep farmers of the Dales.

We remain with the Cistercians at **Byland Abbey**, where a community of white monks finally settled after a long peripatetic existence. The ruins are noted for their surviving patches of medieval tiling which display simple, delicate patterns composed of red, yellow and black. At **Helmsley Castle** we have reached the ancestral home of Walter Espec, founder of Kirkham and Rievaulx, but the extant remains date from the tenure of those de Roos lords who left

The elegant skeleton of Rievaulx Abbey in Yorkshire.

their heraldic signature so boldly emblazoned across the gatehouse at Kirkham, as if underlining the close relationship between the seigneurial and the monastic spheres.

From Helmsley it is but a short distance up Rye Dale to **Rievaulx Abbey** where Walter Espec ended his days as a humble monk. The site was described at the time as 'providing for the monks a kind of second paradise of wooded delights'. This was the first Cistercian house in Yorkshire and the second in England after Waverley in Surrey. The great nave of the church, now stripped of its external cladding and exposed to the heavens, is a Gothic skeleton which reveals all the structural power and inner grace of the style. Rievaulx also shows how the ascetic ideals of the founding fathers were modified as their revenues increased. The rebuilding of the east end of the church in around 1225 displays a degree of flamboyance and decoration at variance with the previous policy of architectural austerity. The religious highpoint at Rievaulx was achieved under Abbot Ailred. At the time of his death in 1167 there were more than six hundred monks and lay brothers at Rievaulx. According to his biographer, the saintly Ailred 'turned the house of Rievaulx into a stronghold for sustaining the weak . . . and those wanderers in the world to whom no house

Exposed to view. *Though **faded** by time, this floor of colourful glazed tiles at Byland Abbey helps remind us of **the** rich interior effect of medieval buildings as originally intended.*

A MOST ROMANTIC RUIN. *In contrast to most well manicured monastic sites, Jervaulx Abbey has been permitted a degree of overgrown abandon. Daisies and buttercups thrive in the former Chapter House.*

The crypt at Lastingham.

of religion gave entrance came to Rievaulx and found the doors open . . . on feast days you might see the church crowded with the brethren like bees in a hive . . .'

Later abbots at Rievaulx led a more worldly existence and lived in baronial style, enjoying all the pleasures that could be purchased with the income from the great flocks of sheep. It has been calculated that the abbey owned as many as 14,000 sheep at the end of the fifteenth century; and there was a diverse range of other profitable activities as well. A superb panoramic view of Rievaulx Abbey may be obtained from a stately terrace on an adjacent hill. This broad sweep of grass following the smooth contours of the slope was carved and levelled by the local landowner Thomas Duncombe in 1713. The lofty scenic promenade was further enhanced for the benefit of this gentleman's refined guests by the clearing of a number of avenues through the woods to open up some magical vistas of the abbey below. The enthusiam for 'Gothick' ruins as picturesque objects in the landscape was in the ascendant. Some of the landed gentry would be building imitation ruins at strategic points in their new parks, but Thomas Duncombe had no need to resort to such artifice with Rievaulx Abbey obligingly in his own backyard.

From these sublime heights we descend underground into a crypt of exceptional interest beneath the church of **St Mary, Lastingham**. This unique early Norman structure with aisles and an apse is virtually a church in its own right. It was built in 1078 on the site of the ancient Celtic monastery founded by St Cedd and St Chad in 659. Note the vigour of the ram's head capitals, carved in typically confident Norman fashion. St Cedd, one of the last of the Celtic evangelisers in eastern England, whom we previously encountered at Bradwell-on-Sea in Essex, ended his days at Lastingham where he fell victim to the plague. There is no visible trace here of St Cedd's original seventh-century monastery, and the present church is dedicated to St Mary, but Lastingham is still venerated as his shrine.

An easterly detour to the coast leads via the remains of **Pickering Castle** to those of **Scarborough Castle** which occupy a truly dramatic site on their rugged cliff headland. This gnarled but defiant pile of ancient masonry watches over the fishing port but appears to hold itself apart from the sprawling seaside resort of much more recent times. There was a dramatic siege here when Piers Gaveston, that much disliked favourite of Edward II, took refuge from his enemies. The assailants coaxed him out of the protective shell of Scarborough Castle with all manner of promises as if teasing a winkle from its shell. But the outcome was a summary execution. The name of Scarborough is derived from the Viking chief Scarthi, a reminder of the Scandinavian harrying of the eastern seaboard over a thousand years ago.

Whitby Abbey, mindless of the Viking threat was founded on an exposed coastal site by St Hilda who lived from 614 to 680. Her mixed community of monks and nuns was eventually raided and wiped out by those vandals of the North Sea, but the memory of St Hilda was still alive when the Benedictines came to Whitby in 1067; and it was the donations of pilgrims at the shrine of St Hilda which financed the magnificent rebuilding of the thirteenth and fourteenth centuries. The present ruins are of this period: the original cells of the seventh century were briefly revealed during the excavation in the 1920s but they now lie concealed under grass just to the north of the nave.

It was during the lifetime of St Hilda that the famous Synod of Whitby was called in 664 by Oswiu, King of Northumbria, to decide whether the Roman or the Celtic version of Christian practice should prevail. The decision to conform to the Roman customs of the rest of Christendom was a truly momentous step towards unity of the Church. The disgruntled adherents of the Celtic persuasion withdrew to Ireland and the western extremities of England, Wales and Scotland. The lead given by Northumbria was soon followed by Mercia and tipped the balance for the whole of England. This is the clearest possible indication of Northumbrian prestige and influence on the national and world stage at the time.

From Whitby we skirt the northern fringes of the North York Moors to arrive at a remarkable Carthusian outpost in what is predominantly Cistercian territory. **Mount Grace Priory** is also exceptional in the clarity of its distinctively Carthusian remains. This monastic order, originating from La Grande Chartreuse in southern France, established the rule of solitary living. Accordingly, each Carthusian monk pledged himself to a hermit-like existence in a separate, individual cell. As may be seen at Mount Grace, the word 'cell' is something of a misnomer for the accommodation consisted of sturdy four-room houses of stone. The ground floor was divided into a living room, bedroom/oratory and study; and the upper floor provided an open space which served as a workshop for activities such as spinning and weaving. Each house had its own walled garden for the monk to grow his vegetables; and at the bottom of the garden lay his individual garderobe. The extent to which privacy and isolation were sought may be gauged by the serving hatches in the thickness of the stone walls. These were built in a right-angled bend in order to avoid the possibility of even casual eye contact between the Carthusian monk and the person serving food. At Mount Grace the outlines of twenty-three such cells have been preserved: fifteen are ranged around three sides of the irregular cloister garth. The effect, as one stands in the middle of the complex surrounded by identical doorways – some still with their secretive serving hatches – is compelling. Here, in its most extreme form we can taste that distinctive blend of

LONELY LIVES. *The Carthusian rule of solitary living produced a distinctive form of monastic architecture. At Mount Grace Priory we see the entrances to the individual cells, each fitted with a serving hatch for meals to be supplied by an unseen hand.*

COMMUNITY ARCHITECTURE. *The communal lifestyle of the great Cistercian houses such as Fountains Abbey called for vast collective structures such as this dormitory undercroft which also accommodated the refectory.*

spiritual isolation and ordered community which is the hallmark of the Carthusians.

However, not all Carthusian monks were able to put up with the enforced solitude required of the Order. Alexander of Lewes, writing in the twelfth century, complained bitterly of Witham in Somerset:

> The whole land is full of communities of monks, and the mutual support provided by the communal life supplies us with a sufficiently good example of religious perfection. Here, alone and without companionship, we become torpid and dull through boredom, seeing no one for days at a time whose example can inspire us, and having only the walls which shut us in to look at.

There must have been many at Mount Grace Priory who would have shared these sentiments.

The journey is punctuated once again by a castle at **Richmond**, perched high on a rocky eminence above the River Swale. Alan the Red, a Breton follower of William the Conqueror, built a great deal of the present castle prior to his death in 1098, but the imposing keep was added in the twelfth century. The castle hall, known as Scolland's Hall, goes back to the time of Alan the Red and is possibly the oldest of its kind in the country. Richmond Castle enjoys a formidable strategic position above the town but there is no record of any great military action; ruin has come through neglect rather than assault.

The road now heads south to another notable Cistercian house at **Jervaulx Abbey**. Its chief delight resides in the romantic overgrown abandon of the ruins where wild flowers set off the grey masonry to much better picturesque effect than the habitual manicured lawns. It was founded by accident by a group of a dozen monks from Byland. Led by John de Kinstan, they managed to get lost in a thick forest, but were guided to safety by a miraculous vision of the Virgin Mary and Child which spoke to the brethren saying: 'Ye are late of Byland but now of Yorevale.' This was interpreted as a clear sign to establish a new community on the spot, remote enough to appeal to the Cistercians. Later, the name of Yorevale was Frenchified to Jervaulx.

At **Middleham Castle** we are once more on territory granted to Alan the Red. He was responsible for the original motte-and-bailey on the site, but the stone keep was built around 1170 by Robert Fitz Ralph. It subsequently became a royal possession under Richard III, but in ensuing centuries the expanding town of Middleham spread into the outer bailey. **Bolton Castle**, on the other hand, still holds itself aloof from its surroundings. This late fourteenth-century rectangular block glowers gaunt and massive over Wensleydale. But by the standards of the day it offered within a high degree of castellar comfort. The private apartments are still intact where Mary Queen of Scots was once held prisoner. Cartloads of personal belongings and luxury furnishings followed her arrival at Bolton Castle on 15 July 1568. The guest apartments of the north-west tower are now without roof or floors; this dank empty shell of moss-covered masonry echoes to the cawing of rooks. Bolton's dungeon is a small chamber hewn out of the solid rock, having much in common with the

The great west range of Fountains Abbey is still essentially intact.

notorious 'pit' favoured by Scottish lairds, into which prisoners were just dropped and forgotten until they died of hunger or fever.

Skipton Castle, at the southern gateway to the Yorkshire Dales, evokes much pleasanter feelings. Snugly ensconced overlooking the town's marketplace it presents to public view the powerful twin towers of its gatehouse. This ensemble owes its elegant crenellation to that great restorer of castles in the seventeenth century, Lady Anne Clifford. The Clifford family motto of 'DESORMAIS' ('henceforth') is spelled out in capital letters of stone tracery crowning the façade like a parapet. Inside, Skipton Castle demonstrates a high degree of excellent preservation work with no trace of modern occupation. The major improvement to the castle were the Tudor apartments which may be admired in the exquisite Conduit Court. This courtyard, beautifully composed around a yew tree planted over 300 years ago by Lady Anne Clifford, has a very special intimacy of scale. Its sense of shelter, peace and containment is especially sweet on those rare hot days of summer in Yorkshire when its shade and cool breezes make it the pleasantest spot in Skipton. On such days it is better not to stop at the normally enchanting ruins of **Bolton Priory** since it now finds itself the centre of a popular country park.

No such fate should ever befall the queen of Yorkshire abbeys, since **Fountains Abbey** is

THE CASTLE AS ROOKERY. *The roofless and floorless north-west tower of Bolton Castle is now occupied by rooks, but the thick masonry, elegant windows and generous fireplaces speak of nobler occupants in times gone by.*

A SHELTERED SPOT. *The charming courtyard of Skipton Castle offers a welcome enclave of protective calm away from the rough extremes of the Yorkshire weather.*

St Wilfrid's Crypt beneath Ripon Cathedral.

under the protection of the National Trust. Set in an exquisite landscape created by the refined gentlefolk of nearby Studley Royal, Fountains usually encourages comparison with paradise. But to its first settlers in 1132, disaffected Benedictines from St Mary's, York, it was perceived as a hostile habitat, 'a place of horror and vast solitude', 'uninhabited for all the centuries back, thick set with thorns, and fit rather to be the lair of wild beasts than the home of human beings'.

The Cistercians rose to the challenge and transformed the scene. The abbey became so popular that it had to be rebuilt almost immediately on a much grander scale at the end of the twelfth century. The architecture tells the familiar tale of rising sophistication. The stark, unadorned simplicity of the nave columns contrasts with the elegant later beauty of the Chapel of the Nine Altars. The size of the establishment is evident in the broad sweep of its western range which appears to embrace the full width of the valley floor. The now roofless dormitory of the lay brethren straddles a spectacular undercroft which served as a refectory and storeroom. One of the last abbots, Marmaduke Huby (1494–1526), built an imposing tower for the abbey church as well as fine new lodgings for himself. At the outset, the Cistercians would never have allowed themselves such ostentation, but times had changed and a high tower became a matter of prestige. Furness Abbey already had one; and Fountains followed suit.

A totally contrasting experience of a much earlier phase of Christianity lies in store at **Ripon**, where beneath the cathedral the original Saxon crypt as built by St Wilfrid around the year 670 is remarkably intact. This is the only part of the church to have survived the destruction meted out by King Eadred of Northumbria in 950; for the kingdom which had summoned the Synod of Whitby had relapsed into paganism. Here in the dark and narrow embrace of Wilfrid's powerful crypt at Ripon you can feel the grip of a simpler, more fundamental Christian vision. By some mystery of acoustics, the chanting of the priest in the cathedral above manages to penetrate the solid, ancient masonry of the crypt, throwing a bridge across the gulf of thirteen centuries.

The road to York is now open, but a halt at **Knaresborough Castle**, looming high above the River Nidd, brings us unexpectedly face to face with one of the four murderers of Thomas Becket, for this was once the home of Sir Hugh de Morville. However, the remains date principally from the fourteenth century.

A good place to enter **York** is through the gate of **Monk Bar** where the road from the north-east pierces the city wall. Look up with respect as you pass through, for high up on the battlemented towers crude but brawny carved figures stand poised to hurl huge boulders on whoever might dare to come to York with any knavish or treacherous purpose in mind. The street pattern of the city within the walls, which has evolved from Roman Eboracum to Anglian Eoforwic and Viking Jorvik, is still almost entirely medieval, although many old buildings have been disguised behind Georgian and Victorian frontages. Yet scratch away the outer skin of many of York's houses and something of at least Tudor vintage will emerge.

The Shambles, with its picturesque cluster of houses, jettied out at odd angles, presents the most authentic view of the medieval streetscape in outline form, but today's sanitised environment has little in common with the stench, squalor and colourful streetlife of the Middle Ages when the Shambles was the centre of the butchers' quarter. The name was derived from the wooden 'shamels' or stalls on which the bleeding carcasses were offered for sale. Waste was probably left to rot in the street or to be carried off by dogs. All medieval cities were unsanitary affairs, but York – according to Edward II – suffered worse than any from 'dung and manure wherewith the streets and lanes are filled and obstructed'.

Royal interest in York at the beginning of the fourteenth century was understandably intense since Edward I, in order to be conveniently located for his Scottish campaigns, had virtually made the city his official capital. In 1298 he moved the entire government to York, until 1304. Kingly concern for the civic amenities is reflected in a fascinating series of ordinances regulating prices and procedures: pigs, prostitutes and all manner of excrement were no longer to be tolerated on the street and four public toilets were to be provided.

York Minster, riding high above the inner city, reflects the passage of royalty in its stained glass and sculpture. In the elaborate choir screen of the 1480s we see portrayed the unfortunate Richard II next to his probable murderer Henry IV, apparently reconciled for all eternity. Forty-one parish churches within the walls once paid tribute to the Minster like a flotilla of yachts to a full-blown galleon; today sixteen remain. Among the many jewels of the Middle Ages, the splendid stained glass of **All Saints** in North Street deserves a special mention. Large stretches of the walls give York a sense of womb-like containment; and the names of the surviving gates roll off the tongue with a satisfying medieval sound: **Bootham Bar**, **Micklegate Bar**, **Monk Bar**, **Fishergate Bar** and **Walmgate Bar**, the last still equipped with its intimidating barbican.

CRIMINALS BEWARE! *This would seem to be the message as you enter York by Monk Bar, where crude figures are poised to drop boulders on any potential troublemakers.*

TO THE GLORY OF GOD. *The majestic beauty of York Minster rises above the medieval houses like a divine apparition.*

Ancient beams of oak in the Merchant Adventurers' Hall in York.

Little remains of the **Abbey of St Mary**, once the wealthiest Benedictine house in the North and the chief ornament of York. But an idea of its former magnificence may be gained from the statuary on display in the Yorkshire Museum which actually sits on the site of the claustral eastern range. There is a spectacular reconstruction of sculptured fragments to represent the vestibule of the chapter house. Full-length figures of the Apostles, angels and one of Moses suggest that this must once have been a lavish gallery of Biblical sculpture. It is thought that the statue of Moses once supported the ribbed vault of the chapter house like a

Gothic caryatid, an extravagance which only the worldly Benedictines would have permitted themselves. In the 1480s an abbot of St Mary's built himself a fine new residence of brick, then newly fashionable; this has been remodelled and now serves as offices to the University of York. Not far from the Yorkshire Museum lies a relic of **St Leonard's Hospital**, founded in 1090 by the Minster clergy. This was one of the largest hospitals in England, intended to relieve the suffering of the urban sick and poor. Only the undercroft remains, in a rather neglected state, hard by a small fragment of the ancient city wall.

York today is virtually landlocked for most practical purposes, but before the tidal River Ouse silted up, the merchants of the city traded by ship across the North Sea with the commercial centres of Scandinavia, Germany and the Low Countries, and as far afield as Spain. Wool, cloth, hides, butter and lead were exported in return for imports of salt, fish, wine, spices and dried fruit. The trade was regulated by the Company of Merchant Adventurers of the City of York which in 1357–61 built the imposing **Merchant Adventurers' Hall**. This building of sturdy beams of oak has been only slightly altered over the past 500 years; and despite its antiquity, it is no mere museum but a working building used for social functions.

One part of York much changed is the area around the castle. This was once moated but today serves as an enormous car park, watched over by the stone edifice of **Clifford's Tower** from the height of its grass-covered 'motte'. An earlier wooden fortification on this very spot was the scene of the bloodiest and most inglorious episode in the annals of medieval York. It was in the year 1190 that there erupted in York one of those antisemitic vendettas which occurred from time to time in all the major cities of England during the early Middle Ages. After some of the leading members of the Jewish community had been murdered by Christian noblemen some 150 of York's Jews fled to the imagined security of the wooden castle. They rapidly saw the hopelessness of their position and concluded a suicide pact, preferring to die by their own hands than by those of their enemies, just as their ancestors had done at Masada when besieged by the Romans in their citadel near the Dead Sea. The following day, happening to be the Sabbath, a handful of survivors were gullible enough to believe promises that they would be spared. On opening the castle gates, they were rapidly put to the sword. Those who owed money to the now non-existent Jewish moneylenders then rushed to York Minster where the documents recording their obligations were stored for safety. The evidence of their debts was burned on the spot in the middle of the nave. With this, it may be assumed that the organisers of this pogrom decided that the affair was over and drifted homewards or back to the taverns whence they had come the previous day. Foul deeds such as this also form part of the legacy of medieval England.

Alabaster is for ever. The exquisite Neville monument at Staindrop.

VII. NORTHUMBRIA AND CUMBRIA

A WEAK AFTERNOON SUN filters through the west window of the parish church of **Staindrop** and falls like a spotlight on the pale alabaster magnificence of Ralph Neville's effigy. This noble figure of the first Earl of Westmorland (1364–1425) lies in the characteristic pose of the pious warrior: hands clasped together in devout prayer, but clad in the elegant plate armour and hood of chain mail of the period, ever ready for battle. The sculptor has taken immense care to carve in their full intricacy the details of the lord's knightly accoutrements. Yet this is no realistic portrayal of a sexagenarian but of a baron in the full vigour of manhood, and with a flowing moustache to emphasise the point. The martial demeanour is heightened by the severed head of a horse which serves Ralph Neville as a pillow. On either side of him, as if in meek and submissive attendance, recline the effigies of his two wives Lady Margaret Stafford and Lady Jane Beaufort, both attired in simple robes of fifteenth-century cut. The presence of both first and second wives seems to suggest that after death the chronology of human life with its neat divisions is totally dissolved, and all loves can co-exist without conflict or taint of polygamy. It was in fact by his second wife, Lady Jane Beaufort, that Ralph Neville sired fourteen children, of whom the youngest daughter married Richard, Duke of York, and was mother to both Edward IV and Richard III.

The Neville family owed their future royal connections to Ralph's timely support for the Lancastrian cause in helping his brother-in-law to the throne as Henry IV. Ralph's father John, Lord Neville, had completed the building of the ancestral stronghold of **Raby Castle** near by. Despite some sumptuous Georgian and Victorian improvements, the external aspect of Raby's west front remains an immensely satisfying and authentically fourteenth-century composition, dominated by the obliquely angled flanking towers of the mighty Neville Gateway.

As we head further north towards the Scottish border, so castles become ever more insistent, spiking the landscape like stone symbols of dynastic ambition. This is a country that has received into its bosom the bleeding bodies of so many slain soldiers over the centuries, not just in the great battles such as Otterburn in 1388 or Flodden in 1513, but in countless minor skirmishes and raids as the cumbersome train of medieval warfare, gaily

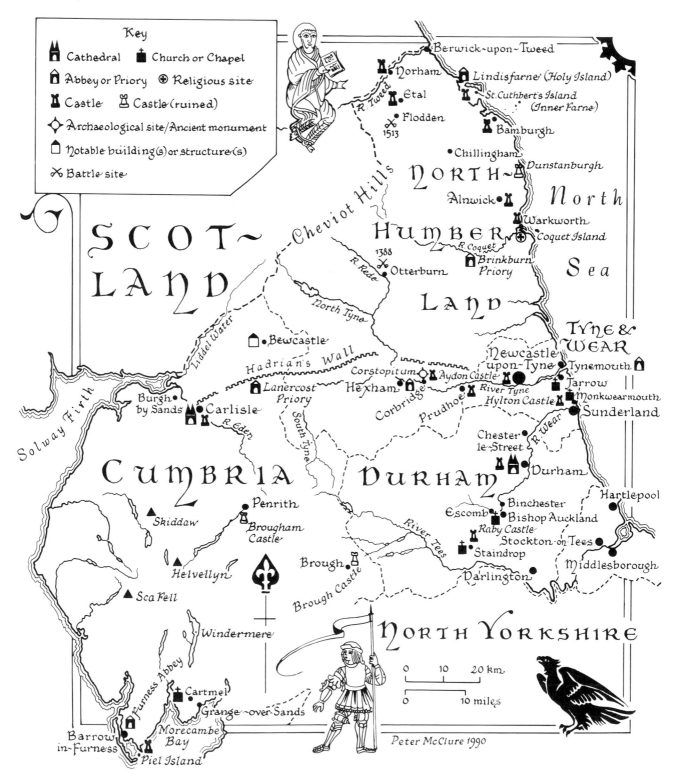

Key

- 🏛 Cathedral
- ✚ Church or Chapel
- 🏠 Abbey or Priory
- ✚ Religious site
- 🏰 Castle
- 🏰 Castle (ruined)
- ◇ Archaeological site/Ancient monument
- ⌂ Notable building(s) or structure(s)
- ✕ Battle site

SCOT~LAND

Berwick-upon-Tweed
Norham
Etal
Flodden
1513
Lindisfarne (Holy Island)
St. Cuthbert's Island
(Inner Farne)
Bamburgh
Chillingham
NORTH~
Dunstanburgh
HUMBER
Alnwick
Warkworth
Coquet Island
Cheviot Hills
1388
Otterburn
R. Coquet
Brinkburn Priory
North Tyne
LAND
North Sea

TYNE & WEAR
Bewcastle
Hadrian's Wall
Corstopitum
Aydon Castle
Newcastle
upon-Tyne
Tynemouth
Hexham
River Tyne
Jarrow
Lanercost Priory
Corbridge
Prudhoe
Hylton Castle
Monkwearmouth
Sunderland
South Tyne
Liddel Water
Burgh
by Sands
Carlisle
R. Eden
R. Wear
Chester
le-Street
Durham

CUMBRIA
DURHAM
Skiddaw
Penrith
Brougham
Castle
Hartlepool
Binchester
Escomb
Bishop Auckland
Helvellyn
River Tees
Raby Castle
Stockton-on-Tees
Brough
Staindrop
Middlesborough
Brough Castle
Darlington
Sca Fell

Windermere
NORTH YORKSHIRE

Furness Abbey
Cartmel
Grange~over~Sands
0   10   20 km
Barrow
in-Furness
Morecambe
Bay
0   10 miles
Piel Island
Peter McClure 1990

pennanted, rumbled on this way and that in the ebb and flow of Anglo-Scottish hostilities. But Northumbria evokes another great medieval theme, equally strong and contrasting as if in direct counterpoint, for this land was also the scene of the inspired spiritual renewal of the seventh century, when Christianity was first preached by the early saints.

In the village of **Escomb** near Bishop Auckland a perfect specimen of a Saxon church has survived to express the austerity and humility of the founding fathers. This is a veritable straitjacket of a church: as you enter, it enfolds you in its tight intimacy. This is a complete antithesis to the broad Gothic vaults of the later Middle Ages. Escomb's strength is rooted in its simplicity and solid construction, offering an immediate sense of comfort and reassurance. But in spite of its homely familiarity, its anonymity in architectural terms is total. The only clues to its estimated date of around 675 lie in the primitive style. It was largely constructed from stones dressed by Roman masons, quarried from the nearby ruins of Binchester; and some still bear Latin inscriptions. One which commemorates the VI Legion has been mounted in the external fabric upside down, as if with the intent of turning history neatly on its head. Northumbria has other early Saxon churches to show, but none is quite so moving and complete as this one at Escomb.

The foundation of Escomb coincided with a momentous event in the life of St Cuthbert, the most revered saint in the entire North of England, who in around the year 676 retired from the monastic community at Lindisfarne to live as a hermit on the remote island of Inner Farne. We shall catch up with the living Cuthbert later on at Lindisfarne Priory on Holy Island, but as we approach the city of **Durham** we are confronted more immediately with the wanderings and final resting place of Cuthbert's cadaver. To the monks of Lindisfarne the holy relics of St Cuthbert were their most precious possession; and when in 875 the community resolved to leave Holy Island, which lay horribly exposed to the increasing depredations of the Viking raiders, they disinterred the saint's coffin and took it with them on their long and complex peregrination in search of a new and secure home. Cuthbert's bones thus embarked on a circuitous journey via Norham, to Whithorn in south-west Scotland, down to Crayke and Ripon in Yorkshire, to Chester-le-Street, and finally in 995 after 120 years of nomadic exile they were brought to a high and rocky escarpment commanding a dramatic bend in the River Wear. Here the monks founded a church and created the basis from which the future city of Durham was to spring.

There was to be just one more journey for Cuthbert: in the panic of the immediate aftermath of the Norman Conquest the monks scuttled back with the relics to their original home at Lindisfarne, but they soon returned to Durham and deposited them where they have lain ever since. Such was the popular appeal of the cult of St Cuthbert that in 1093 a mighty Norman cathedral was commenced to replace the lowly Saxon church. Thus it might be claimed that the Romanesque masterpiece of **Durham Cathedral** sprang essentially from the bones of St Cuthbert. Here at Durham the sheer weight, power and permanence of the Norman style are hugely impressive. The massive columns with their deeply incised patterns

LOWLY SAXON. *The modesty of style and smallness of scale give the Saxon church at Escomb a particular poignancy. It is a product of the very community it was designed to serve.*

MIGHTY NORMAN. *Durham Cathedral, soaring dramatically over the River Wear, conveys a message of temporal as well as spiritual power. This was the architectural expression of the new order and its culture.*

of chevron, spirals and diamond march resolutely through the nave towards the east end where the much travelled mortal remains of Cuthbert lie buried beneath a simple slab behind the high altar.

Not content with this prestigious set of relics as a lure for pilgrims, the enterprising Earlfred of Durham made off around 1020 with the bones of the Venerable Bede, crudely purloined from their proper resting place at Jarrow. They are now interred in the Galilee Chapel at the west end of Durham Cathedral, so that Bede and Cuthbert – the two great Christian figures of the Saxon North – now form the two poles of the cathedral, creating as strong an axis of spirituality as could be imagined. The Galilee Chapel is a curious structure: the human scale is an effective foil to the titanic nave, but the insistence of the jagged dogtooth decoration can be rather disturbing. In the Cathedral Treasury are displayed fragments of Cuthbert's seventh-century oak coffin with linear carvings of archaic simplicity portraying Christ and the Apostles. There is also an exquisite jewelled pectoral cross, which seems at variance with the austerity of Cuthbert's life, and the finely embroidered stole, maniple and girdle which were placed in the tenth-century grave. The Treasury also contains the magnificent lion's head bronze knocker from the north door of the cathedral. It is thought to be of mid-twelfth century date and to have been used by those wishing to invoke the medieval right of sanctuary.

The city of Durham is completely dominated by its cathedral; and the famous vista has not been better described than by the romantic nineteenth-century poet Sir Walter Scott, whose verses have been mounted on a plaque on Prebend's Bridge:

> Grey towers of Durham
> Yet well I love thy mixed and massive piles
> Half church of God. Half castle 'gainst the Scot.
> And long to roam these venerable aisles
> With records stored of deeds long since forgot.

The cathedral shares the hilltop with the castle, which was held by the Bishop of Durham who ruled the North as a viceroy of the Conqueror, a military magnate as much as a cleric. Castle and cathedral together form a tight medieval enclave, strongly reminiscent of a French *cité*. The period atmosphere is heightened by steep narrow passages which penetrate the rocky fastness of the citadel, with appropriately forbidding names such as Windy Gap and Dark Entry, where human beings feel small and crushed beneath the weight of so much ancient masonry on all sides.

There is a return to the smaller, Saxon scale of things at the church of **St Peter, Monkwearmouth** where Bede served as a novice before moving on to Jarrow. Only the square tower and part of the west wall survive of this very important early Christian monument. There is more to be seen at **St Paul's, Jarrow**, one of the most renowned sites of Saxon Christianity, since it became home in 685 to the Venerable Bede, the foremost scholar and historian of his day. It was at Jarrow that Bede compiled his monumental *Ecclesiastical History of the English Peoples*. The monastery where he laboured at his task has not survived as a structure above ground, but we can imagine him with inky quill scratching over parchment, often writing by the spluttering light of tallow candles, his fingers quite numb from the cold winter winds from icy Scandinavia. The monastic buildings were probably only slightly better than the primitive housing of the age. Out of such inauspicious surroundings did Bede and other scholars make Jarrow a focal point of religious learning in Europe long centuries before any Oxford college was founded.

Saxon windows at St Paul's, Jarrow.

The dedication stone of St Paul's may be seen high up in the chancel arch. It dates the church to 685, the year of Bede's move to Jarrow. There is a dubious relic in the shape of a roughly fashioned wooden seat, which has come to be known as Bede's Chair. However, it cannot be dated back far enough to qualify as the real seat of the saintly scholar. Authentic enough, on the other hand, is the fabric of the chancel which contains two original Saxon windows with characteristic rounded stone lintels like raised eyebrows over the circular lights. One of these contains some fragments of stained glass manufactured in the monastery's own workshop. These pieces of blue, orange and yellow are recognised as the oldest examples of stained glass in Europe. There is something awesome in the contemplation of these simple colours, still burning bright after more than thirteen hundred years.

Tynemouth Priory on the north side of the River Tyne introduces a rather different note, characteristic of the declining years of the Middle Ages. The fifteenth-century chapel, known as the **Percy Chantry**, is a small structure but its vault is crowded with a profusion of intersecting stone ribs which sport thirty-three separate stone bosses. By such architectural extravagance did the Percy family conspire to achieve a remission on purgatory. Henceforth,

THE RICH MAN IN HIS CASTLE. *Northumbria abounds in finely built and well appointed castles. Raby Castle* (above) *offers a splendid medieval frontage. Prudhoe Castle* (right) *proposes a more intimate version of the castellar lifestyle.*

it will be impossible to avoid the Percys' ubiquitous presence in their ancestral lands to the north, and their family crest is emblazoned already on the main front of **Hylton Castle**, some miles to the south near Sunderland, probably as a diplomatic gesture of the owner to invoke their goodwill and protection.

Heading inland along the banks of the Tyne, it is worth braving the modern conurbation of **Newcastle** to seek out the late Norman interior of the Castle keep, built in around 1170 just before the Gothic style was to sweep all before it. Further upstream we come to **Prudhoe Castle**, which once controlled strategic routes through Northumberland. The castle's first owners were the Umfravilles, but in 1381 the omnipresent Percys acquired Prudhoe through a marriage alliance and conspired to retain it through the centuries. The castle is a small but serious affair, entered via a barbican and over the moat to a sturdy gatehouse. A horseman would have felt swallowed up by the barbican, totally at the mercy of the garrison, and perhaps even intimidated by the reverberation of his own horse's hooves under the stone vault, before being disgorged into the inner courtyard. More homely is **Aydon Castle** nearby, which is really less of a castle than a fortified manor with a pleasingly domestic feel about it. The overriding necessity for defence in this part of the country is witnessed by the tower house of the **Vicar's Pele, Corbridge**. Evidently the lawlessness of the local raiders did not spare gentlemen of the cloth from the threat of violent assault and harassment.

Hexham Abbey, just a few miles further up the Tyne, survived the ravages of the Dissolution to remain in service as a parish church. At the west end of the nave there ascends a wondrously preserved night stair. This originally permitted access directly from the 'dorter' of the monastery to the church for the monks attending those offices – usually Matins and Lauds – held during the hours of nightly rest. It is easy to imagine the familiar scene of a cold, dark church lit by flickering candles as the monks filed down the night stair, still half asleep and trying to maintain some body warmth by wrapping their coarse woollen habits tightly about themselves. On such occasions the plainsong chanting and praying must have been accomplished in a state of only partial consciousness.

A less obvious stairway gives access from the north transept down to the crypt which formed part of the Saxon church founded in 674 by St Wilfrid, just a few years after his church at Ripon. Here the re-use of Roman masonry, already noted at Escomb, is even more apparent. Quarried from the ruins of Corstopitum near Corbridge, the stones show not only the occasional inscription but many instances of decorative tooling of the highest order, with delicate cable, leaf and berry, and billet mouldings much in evidence. Although St Wilfrid himself had seen the fine architecture of Rome, the Saxon builders were probably blind to the artistic merits of the stones, for they arranged them at random. As at Ripon, the crypt offers a slightly claustrophobic experience; and one wonders what it must have been like in the semi-darkness amidst the crush of pilgrims pressing to touch the shrine or saintly relics which may have been kept there.

Happier feelings are stimulated by the sight of **Brinkburn Priory** which occupies one of the most romantic settings of all monastic houses. The approach is down a steep and wooded slope which conceals the church until the last moment when the north door suddenly appears, framed picturesquely by trees and rhododendron bushes. The church is roofed but empty of furniture, so that full play is given to the powerful architecture within which marks the transition from the round Norman to the pointed Gothic arch. This secluded spot by a bend of the River Coquet must have been cherished by successive generations of Augustinians during the four centuries of the community's existence here from foundation in 1135 to dissolution in 1536.

Steps leading up to Warkworth Hermitage.

We are now entering the heartland of Percy territory at **Warkworth Castle**, where the same River Coquet approaches tidal waters before spilling out into the North Sea. The castle has undergone many different building phases, from its birth as a primitive motte-and-bailey which was then strengthened by a stone curtain wall in the twelfth century and endowed with a magnificent stylish keep in the early fifteenth century. This last structure, though somewhat altered and restored, still conveys the essence of a truly luxurious, late medieval, lordly habitation. The noble keep in the shape of a Greek Cross bears the rampant Percy Lion sculpted large on the centre bay of its north front. In terms of its domestic comfort this building represents a quantum leap from the dark and cramped accommodation of even princely houses in the Middle Ages. Here, all is light, space and orderly planning, together with some sophisticated technical devices such as a central lantern in the roof and a clever drainage system which channelled rainwater from the gutters through concealed conduits down to the kitchens where it could be used for cooking or just washing the floor. But despite its amenities Warkworth was not a happy place in the Percy family saga, for it was

THE NIGHT STAIR. *Well worn steps at Hexham Abbey where generations of monks have shuffled back and forth between their dormitory and the church.*

THE LATEST IN CULINARY CONVENIENCE. *The kitchens at Warkworth Castle represented the state of the art in the early fifteenth century. Special features included conduits to channel rainwater from the roof of the keep to a large cistern.*

Part of the medieval fabric at Alnwick Castle.

here that the ill-fated plot was hatched against Henry IV, which led to the defeat and death of the impetuous Harry Hotspur at Shrewsbury in 1403. Shakespeare set three scenes of *Henry IV, Part I* within the walls of Warkworth Castle.

Just around a long bend of the River Coquet, and now accessible only by boat, lies **Warkworth Hermitage**, a jewel of a chapel hewn out of the living rock of the cliff, as were many other isolated hermits' refuges at the time. What makes this one exceptional is the supreme mastery of the architectural carving which perfectly imitates the vaults, columns and arches of a Gothic structure. The living accommodation of the hermit-priest was grafted on to the rock and has since become ruinous, but the chapel within is in immaculate condition but for some weathering of the carved detail. It contains a curious sculpture in the arched recess of the south window, which has been interpreted as a portrayal of the Nativity, showing the Virgin Mary reclining with the Infant Jesus lying on her breast. Although much eroded by the elements, this work of simple piety is still deeply moving, and adds a special aura to one of the most mysterious of medieval sites in the whole of England. The waters of the River Coquet have helped keep this place remote and inviolate over the years; and the short crossing in a rowing boat conveys the sense of a real voyage back in time.

The exact date of the foundation of the Warkworth Hermitage is unknown, but it was most probably the pious act of one of the fourteenth-century Percy lords of the nearby castle. But it was **Alnwick Castle** which became the main seat of the Percys; and it was the Percy first Duke of Northumberland who renovated and extended the accommodation at Alnwick in the eighteenth century, employing the illustrious architect and designer Robert Adam. Further work was carried out in the nineteenth century for the fourth Duke by Anthony Salvin, so that what one sees today is largely a picturesque vision woven around the original medieval castle. The great octagonal towers built by Henry, second Lord Percy of Alwick, around 1350, which flank the entrance to the keep, are now devoid of any martial presence. But even in its present role as a romantic ensemble, it is no less impressive. The battlements, both real and mock, are crowded with menacing statues, ancient and modern. The whole is a curious blend of authentic and bogus medievalism, set in a park landscape contrived by Capability Brown.

Further up the coast **Dunstanburgh Castle** is the genuine article, but at the expense of remaining a ruin. This was once the possession of John of Gaunt in his capacity as Lieutenant of the Marches. The castle is located on a spur of land jutting out into the sea. At times it seems to have detached itself entirely and to float in a haze, more like a projected image than a real structure of weight and substance.

Bamburgh Castle is an even more dramatic sight, a rambling citadel on what was once the fortress of Ida, a sixth-century King of Bernicia, which was later merged into the resplendent Kingdom of Northumbria. The oldest part of the castle is the great Norman keep by Henry II, which has been overwhelmed by later additions. Lindisfarne Castle, which forms an effective counterpoint to Bamburgh across the waters on Holy Island, is perhaps the most enigmatic of Northumberland's castles. It is essentially a twentieth-century Edwardian creation by that master architect Edwin Lutyens, wrapped around a sea castle of 1549. Thus it has no claim to a real medieval origin, but it has a strength of composition which would have been totally at home in the Middle Ages: it seems to grow out of the rock and to possess all the threat and power of a mailed, clenched fist raised in defiance to the sky.

In fact, the first castle was built with stone plundered from the abandoned **Lindisfarne Priory** immediately after the Dissolution. The monastic ruins on view today are of the twelfth-century church and the thirteenth-century ancillary buildings of the Benedictine refoundation of 1083. But the real significance of Lindisfarne, of which there are sadly no visible remains, goes back to the monastery founded here in 635 by St Aidan, an Irish monk from Columba's community on Iona, who was summoned by King Oswald of Northumbria to spread the Gospel among his people. The choice of an island site was typical of the rigorous Celtic regime of austerity and solitude. Yet the Holy Island of Lindisfarne was, as Bede described it, not totally cut off: 'As the tide ebbs and flows, this place is surrounded twice daily by the waves of the sea like an island, and twice, when the sands are dry, it becomes again attached to the mainland.'

Under Aidan and his successors Lindisfarne became a bright light in the North; and the fame of the place was further enhanced by the life of Cuthbert, who withdrew from the community for a hermit's life on the tiny islet, now known in his honour as **St Cuthbert's Isle**, a merest wisp of land separated only by the tides from Holy Island itself. Cuthbert's yearning for solitude then took him to a more isolated spot on **Inner Farne**, a real island some distance away. Then in 685 he was reluctantly persuaded to return to Lindisfarne to take up the appointment as Bishop. However, this was already the eventide of Cuthbert's

HOLY ISLAND. *Lindisfarne's quasi-insular location offered no protection from the Viking raiders; and nothing remains of the original monastery. The ruins of the priory church date from the twelfth century, long after the death of St Cuthbert.*

CISTERCIAN ARCHITECTURAL INDULGENCE. *At Furness Abbey the once austere 'white monks' embarked on an ambitious and ostentatious rebuilding of their establishment in the rich red sandstone of the region.*

life; and, realising that his end was near, he withdrew once more to the Inner Farne, where he died in 687. His body was brought back to Lindisfarne for burial.

There the story of Cuthbert might have ended, as just another saintly figure beckoning across the centuries, but his physical life was really no more than a prelude to the Cuthbert story which unfolded after his death. In 698 the monks of Lindisfarne disinterred Cuthbert's earthly remains and discovered that his body was still remarkably fresh even after eleven years of burial. It was then reburied in the oak coffin, of which fragments may be seen in the Treasury of Durham Cathedral. As the word spread of the miraculous preservation of Cuthbert's body, so the relics acquired tremendous fame and prestige. Pilgrims flocked to Lindisfarne and boosted the revenues of the monastery. It is thought that the wonderfully illuminated Lindisfarne Gospels were created soon after the re-interment as an artistic response to the rising glory and wealth of Lindisfarne.

Increased riches were a mixed blessing for Lindisfarne in the eighth century since the monastery became a quick and easy prize for the Viking raiders who were poised to devastate the eastern seaboard of England. In 793 the Scandinavian scourge descended on Lindisfarne. The horrific visitation was dramatically recorded in the *Anglo-Saxon Chronicle* at that time:

> In this terrible year portents appeared over Northumbria, and miserably frightened the inhabitants: these were exceptional flashes of lightning, and fiery dragons were seen flying through the air . . . and in the same year the harrying of the heathen miserably destroyed God's church in Lindisfarne by rapine and slaughter.

There is in the museum at Lindisfarne a fragment of a stone carving which portrays a serried mass of armed warriors, most probably a stylised rendering of Viking marauders.

The community rebuilt, but eventually decided to look for a safer home for themselves and Cuthbert's relics. Thus began in 875 the long journey which was to end in Durham. At Norham, one of the stages in Cuthbert's posthumous odyssey, a castle was built in the twelfth century on a steep ravine overlooking the River Tweed by a bishop of Durham. The defensive potential of the site which had appealed to the monks was evidently recognised also by the Bishops Palatine, to whom the Norman kings entrusted a policing role in the North. **Norham Castle** was the venue of an English parliament summoned in 1291 by Edward I to determine the Scottish succession, disputed by Robert Bruce and John Balliol. This is one of the mightiest of the many fortifications which bristle along the Anglo-Scottish border. Another fine essay in the art of defensive architecture is **Etal Castle**, one of those compact border towers, consisting principally of a square four-storey keep contained within a curtain wall. At **Berwick-upon-Tweed**, which has changed hands several times in the tug-of-war between English and Scots, the original fortifications built by Edward I have largely disappeared beneath the striking sixteenth-century artillery bastions and ramparts. An impressive stretch of the Edwardian defences may still be seen beyond the railway station which was actually built on the site of the castle.

In Northumberland, there is one final and curious relic of the Middle Ages which has conspired to survive as a piece of living history. The herd of wild, white cattle at **Chillingham** is the only species in the country not to have been crossed with any domestic strain. For at least 700 years the cattle have been left to their own devices to roam over a part of Northumberland in a natural habitat that has inevitably shrunk in the course of time, but which is now safeguarded at just over 300 acres. It is quite possible that their ancestry goes back to the aurochs which were native to Britain long before the Romans introduced their own domestic breed. Thus the Chillingham cattle are as authentic a part of the medieval scene as any castle or cathedral; and their rural landscape has been left untouched as well. Unlike their

Norham Castle's imposing keep.

passive domestic cousins, these wild cattle do not accept the presence of man and will not allow themselves to be approached, even for veterinary inspection; and they will only eat grass or hay from their own meadow. These animals are thus obstinately independent of all the devices of twentieth-century civilisation. They run their own affairs, regulate their own numbers – which currently stand at about fifty – and, in short, will have no truck whatsoever with mankind. With their distinctive horns and disdainful demeanour they stand, or even conspire to sit aloof, confident in their own antiquity and ability to resist change.

East-west communications across the north country have always been difficult. This was especially so in the Middle Ages and things have not essentially changed that much. It is still necessary to make a detour through southern Scotland or to return south as far as the Tyne valley in order to cross from Northumberland to Cumbria. This latter ancient route was transformed by the Roman builders of Hadrian's Wall into Britain's first fortified frontier, and today links the cities of Newcastle and Carlisle. However, it is worth making a northerly deviation, before descending on Carlisle, to the tiny Cumbrian village of **Bewcastle**, for it shelters in its churchyard the shaft of an outstanding early Christian high cross, which ranks as a masterpiece of Saxon carving. The Anglian cross head itself is missing; and the

A ROOM WITH A VIEW. *The ruinous state of Brough Castle has opened up a panoramic vista of the Cumbrian countryside. The ruins were restored by Lady Anne Clifford in the seventeenth century.*

PICTURESQUE PERFECTION. *Brougham Castle, just outside Penrith on a lovely river bank, presents a scenic rather than martial character. It also received the attention of Lady Anne Clifford.*

Carlisle Castle's forbidding gatehouse.

remaining shaft, 14 foot 6 inches high, would originally have been painted in garish colours, presenting an inspirational sight as striking as a totempole.

Narrow roads drop down from the hills to the valley floor where the pastoral setting of **Lanercost Priory** belies a turbulent past when the monastic peace was regularly shattered by raids from across the Scottish border. This house of Augustinian canons was founded in the twelfth century by the de Vaux family; some of their tombs may be seen in the parish church which has taken over the nave of the priory. Lanercost found itself in the crossfire of the Anglo-Scottish wars, suffering assaults from both William Wallace and Robert Bruce. Edward I, the 'Hammer of the Scots' stayed three times at Lanercost; and it was not far from this spot, at Burgh-on-Sands overlooking the Solway Firth, that he died at the age of sixty-eight. Although weak from dysentery, he was still pursuing his enemy Robert Bruce of Scotland with his last reserves of energy. According to a pleasing local tradition, evensong at Lanercost Priory is held with the sole illumination of candles, creating a world of deep, flitting shadows and dancing flames that would still be familiar to the Augustinian canons.

Although the city walls have long since been demolished **Carlisle Castle** serves to recall that this was England's most northerly outpost on the west coast during the wars with Scotland. But it is a small detail of the castle which claims our attention: within the keep a large section of the wall has been covered with decorative carvings of an endearing if crude execution. There is a naked lady transfixed by arrows, presumably of desire; and, all crowded in on one another, a mermaid, helmed warriors in hand-to-hand combat and a heavily armoured St George standing triumphantly on the dragon which he has just slain. This curious sculptural gallery was created, or so it was thought, by prisoners to while away the boredom of their incarceration, but opinion has now swung in favour of the guards as the anonymous artists.

Carlisle Cathedral forms the other medieval pole of the city. Its castellated tower is symptomatic of Carlisle's embattled position. In the choir there is an imposing wagon roof which was repainted in the nineteenth century with a striking design of golden stars against a deep blue sky: a notable piece of Victorian medievalism. Much older painting survives in the genuinely medieval screens which illustrate the lives of St Anthony, St Augustine and St Cuthbert. These are not of the highest artistic merit, but they are an authentic glimpse of how religious stories were communicated through the medieval equivalent of cartoon strips to a largely illiterate public. Art critics should not judge them too harshly.

In central Cumbria the castles at **Brougham** and **Brough** have more in common than similarities in name. Both belong to the category of picturesque ruins, the former sitting snugly by the River Eamont outside Penrith and the latter on a lofty crag overlooking the ancient route that is now used by the A66. In the seventeenth century both castles were in the possession of the remarkable Lady Anne Clifford, whose enthusiasm for the Middle Ages went way beyond the restoration of ancient buildings. Indeed, she pushed her medievalist fantasy to the extent of forcing her entire household on occasions to experience the domestic conditions of their twelfth-century ancestors.

In the south of Cumbria, the Priory Church of St Mary the Virgin at **Cartmel** was rescued long after the Dissolution for use as a parish church, but the magnificent ruins of **Furness Abbey** have been left unimproved. At the time of the Dissolution, this was the second richest Cistercian house in the whole of England. The wealth of the establishment is readily apparent in the excellence of the architecture in mellow red sandstone. Furness Abbey provides yet another telling example of the Cistercian shift away from austerity to artistic embellishment. In the south wall of the presbytery there are an intricately carved sedilia and piscina of the fifteenth century; the mid-thirteenth-century chapter house has the spartan twin lancets of the period, but elaborate medallions have been mounted above them. Most ostentatious of all was the west tower for the belfry added in 1500. This great structure, much of which remains, sports projecting buttresses with niches for statues under elaborately gabled canopies. Equally impressive at Furness are the practical arrangements: the stream has been divided and diverted into several separate channels in order to supply and cleanse all parts of the monastic complex.

But life was not without its threats, for the Abbot of Furness in the fourteenth century saw fit to build himself a stout castle on tiny Piel Island to the south. **Piel Castle** was intended to serve both as a bolt-hole in times of trouble as well as a lookout and deterrent against seaborne raiders from the north. The view south-east from Piel Island encompasses the flat expanse of Morecambe Bay. This is a moody spot, conducive to a few moments of medieval reverie. There is little here to remind us of the twentieth century; and even the mighty Blackpool Tower across the waters shows up as the merest pimple on the distant shoreline of Lancashire.

A remarkable group of sculpture at Malmesbury Abbey.

VIII. WESSEX

ALMESBURY, ENJOYING A CURIOUSLY detached location in that vague interspace to the south of the Cotswolds but belonging to the far north of Wiltshire, is one of the most venerable of medieval towns in England, going back at least to the seventh century. At the time of the Dissolution its ancient Benedictine abbey was quickly turned into a textile workshop and became a forerunner of industrial production. This dramatic change of use was noted by John Leland when he visited the town in the early 1540s: 'The hole logginges of thabbay be now longging to one Stumpe, an exceding riche clothiar that boute them of the king ... At this present tyme every corner of the vaste houses of office that belongid to thabbay be fulle of lumbes to weve cloth yn.' But William Stumpe was not without a social conscience, as Leland also tells us that 'This Stumpe was the chef causer and contributer to have thabbay chirch made a paroch chirch.' It is recorded that he presented the nave of the abbey church to the people of Malmesbury on 20 August 1541 because their existing parish church of St Paul was in a ruinous condition. In fact, only the tower and steeple of St Paul's now remain standing, just across from the abbey itself.

Apart from the fine Norman nave, the rest of **Malmesbury Abbey** has sunk into a state of advanced dilapidation, but there is enough within this truncated remnant to stir the imagination. But before entering, we must reinstate in the mind's eye the missing spire which rose from the crossing of the church to a height reputedly greater than that of Salisbury Cathedral. At the end of the fifteenth century it fell victim to a violent storm which wrecked the east end of the church; and the tower at the west end collapsed two centuries later, taking with it the three western bays of the nave. But even in its present lopped and shorn condition the nave of Malmesbury Abbey still dominates the town from its lofty summit like a mutilated leviathan.

The south porch of the abbey presents itself as a conventional Norman portal framed by a series of round arches vibrant with carved mouldings, but once inside the porch there comes into view a splendid tympanum above the inner door representing Christ in Majesty; and there, high up on either side, are two semicircular panels showing the Apostles in full relief, divided into two groups of six, each with a flying angel to grace the scene. The architectural

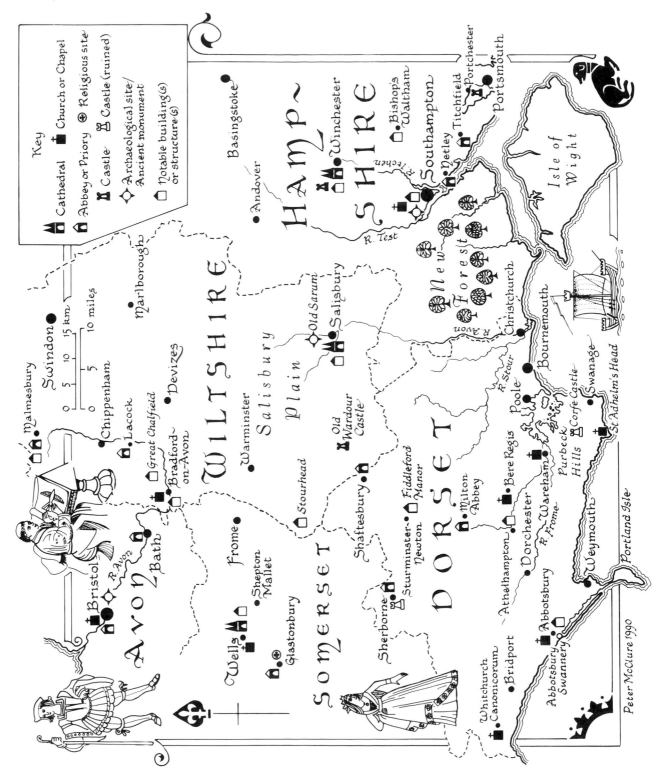

Key

♙ Cathedral
✝ Church or Chapel
🛡 Abbey or Priory   ⊕ Religious site
Ⅺ Castle   Ⅱ Castle (ruined)
◇ Archaeological site/ Ancient monument
▢ Notable building(s) or structure(s)

HAMP~SHIRE

Basingstoke
Andover
Winchester
Bishop's Waltham
Southampton
Netley
Titchfield
Portchester
Portsmouth
Isle of Wight
R. Itchen
R. Test

New Forest
Christchurch
Bournemouth
R. Avon

WILTSHIRE
Marlborough
Swindon
Malmesbury
Chippenham
Lacock
Devizes
Great Chalfield
Bradford~on-Avon
Warminster
Salisbury Plain
Old Sarum
Salisbury
Old Wardour Castle
Stourhead

10 miles
15 km
10
5
5
0
0

AVON
Bristol
R. Avon
Bath

SOMERSET
Frome
Shepton Mallet
Wells
Glastonbury

DORSET
Shaftesbury
Sturminster Newton
Fiddleford Manor
Milton Abbey
Sherborne
Bere Regis
Athelhampton
Dorchester
Wareham
R. Frome
R. Stour
Poole
Purbeck Hills
Corfe Castle
Swanage
St. Adhelm's Head
Weymouth
Portland Isle
Whitchurch Canonicorum
Bridport
Abbotsbury
Abbotsbury Swannery

Peter McClure 1990

framework is undoubtedly Norman, but the figurative carving has an unmistakable Saxon quality in its tender lines. Whatever its exact cultural parentage, this tripartite sculptural group is among the most artistic and moving of its kind in England. It is indeed miraculous that it has survived the iconoclasm of both the Reformation and the Puritans.

Inside the church, in the north aisle, there lies a most remarkable tomb and effigy of the Saxon King Athelstan, grandson of Alfred the Great. The tomb chest is medieval and the head of the effigy as well as the lion at its feet are probably even later, but the cloaked body of the king is much older. This is a precious link with the pre-Conquest origins of Malmesbury Abbey; but even this does not take us right back to the original foundation of a hermitage by the seventh-century Irish monk Maidulph and the monastery built on the spot by King Ine of Wessex, whose nephew St Aldhelm (c.639–709) became the first Abbot of Malmesbury. Aldhelm, later Bishop of Sherborne, was recognised throughout Europe as an inspired writer; and some four centuries later he was followed by a worthy literary emulator in the person of the famous William of Malmesbury (c.1090–1143), one of the greatest of medieval historians, who declined the position as abbot in order not to prejudice his scholarly pursuits.

William, Aldhelm and Maidulph are all commemorated in modern stained-glass windows along with a fourth worthy of Malmesbury, a certain Elmer, known as 'the flying monk', and arguably as the first British aeronaut for his eleventh-century attempt at human flight. According to William of Malmesbury's account, Elmer launched himself from the church tower and flew 'for more than the distance of a furlong; but agitated by the violence of the wind and the current of air, as well as by the consciousness of his rash attempt, he fell and broke his legs.' Apparently, Elmer put his failure down to the lack of a tail rather than to the quality of his artificial wings.

The associations at Malmesbury Abbey are indeed rich and diverse. As for the town, it was one of Alfred the Great's fortified 'burhs', those ninth-century units of civil defence against any counter-offensive by the Danes. As you leave the abbey precinct, the entrance to the town is marked by a magnificent market cross, which was newly built when John Leland described it some 450 years ago: 'There is a right fair and costely peace of worke in the market place made al of stone and curiusly voultid for poore market folkes to stande dry when rayne cummith.' This charming structure still provides valuable shelter to pedestrians caught in a shower.

A fascinating contrast to Malmesbury Abbey is provided by the very different fate of **Lacock Abbey**, originally founded by Countess Ela of Salisbury in 1232 as an upper-class nunnery, of which she became the abbess in 1241. The superb fifteenth-century cloister and the thirteenth-century sacristy, chapter house and warming room beneath the nuns' dormitory have survived intact within the remodelled shell of an eighteenth-century country house, designed by that great exponent of the early Gothic Revival, Sanderson Miller. This amateur architect acquired quite a reputation for producing anything 'Gothick', even

THE HIDDEN CLOISTER. *The rebuilding of Lacock Abbey in Wiltshire as a private residence conserved the original cloistered quadrangle of the Benedictine nunnery.*

A SAXON CHURCH REDISCOVERED. *The late Saxon church of St Laurence at Bradford-on-Avon was only identified in the mid-nineteenth century thanks to the efforts of an antiquarian priest.*

'ready-made ruins'. Unlike other monastic conversions, Lacock Abbey works happily as an overall composition, despite some physical dislocation between the fabric of the various periods. Fitting tribute is paid to the spirit of the parent building; and this tradition was also maintained by the nineteenth-century remodelling of the south front which created a gallery lit by three seemingly medieval oriel windows. Countess Ela would still feel at home here.

This woman was the very model of the pious lady and a noble example of conjugal fidelity. The awkward situation she found herself in must have been shared by countless other wives during the Middle Ages. Her husband William Longespee, half-brother of Richard I and John, had been absent abroad in pursuance of his baronial duty for so long that hopeful suitors began pressing Ela for her hand in marriage, claiming that her husband must surely be dead. The Countess rejected them all, saying that she had seen a vision of his safe return, which in due course was happily fulfilled. When her husband eventually died, Ela founded Lacock Abbey to his memory along with the Carthusian house at Hinton in Somerset.

Near by, at **Great Chalfield**, still enjoying a remote rural location, there stands a manor house of immense charm, which dates back to the fourteenth century at least. However, most of what one sees today was the work of Thomas Tropnell in the 1460s and 70s. The Great Hall still occupies the centre of the house, but no trace has been discovered of the dais, or elevated platform, which by tradition would have accommodated the lord's high table. The absence of this medieval feature might be explained by the presence of an entirely separate dining room, an innovation in its day, where the master of the house and his family could enjoy their meals in privacy away from the public scrutiny of their retinue of staff and servants. Behind the later panelling of this cosy dining room there is a wall painting of a powerful figure (with five fingers on each hand as well as a thumb) who has been identified as Thomas Tropnell, the main builder of Great Chalfield. There he broods, although faded by time, seated in a chair, still watching over meals like a ghost at a banquet. No wonder that he was panelled over in around 1550 by John Eyre.

The town of **Bradford-on-Avon** climbs up the steep hillsides which hem in the River Avon, a watercourse which provided the energy for the textile mills that were the mainstay of the place well into the eighteenth century. The streetscape is predominantly post-medieval, but there are – besides the parish church – two buildings which would merit a place in any selection of England's best architecture from the Middle Ages. Just across the road from the Church of the Holy Trinity there stands the remarkable Saxon **Church of St Laurence**, a thousand-year-old treasure, whose identity was only recognised as recently as 1871 by the vicar Canon Jones, a resourceful amateur antiquarian. Thanks to his intervention, this delightful and stylish church was coaxed back into life from its partition into a school and a dwelling, which had been further disguised by a profusion of ivy. The whole church has now been skilfully restored; and it ranks as one of the best of all Saxon churches on account both of its quality and lack of later remodelling. Its upper parts have been dated to around 950 to 1000, but its lower walls may be those of an original foundation by St

Aldhelm, who, according to William of Malmesbury, built the *ecclesiola* or little church. In a part of England especially rich in bright, generously proportioned churches of Perpendicular Gothic, St Laurence with its dim and narrow interior offers a taste of a much earlier version of church architecture.

Bradford-on-Avon's other medieval jewel is the **Great Barn**, built by the abbey at Shaftesbury to receive the tithes of produce from the land it owned in the district. In terms of style and stature it comes a close second to that other splendid tithe barn at Great Coxwell in Oxfordshire. Another utilitarian structure of note is the town bridge, which has retained two of its

The Great Barn, Bradford-on-Avon, Wiltshire.

thirteenth-century pointed arches on the eastern side. The rest is seventeenth-century, including the curious addition grafted to one of its piers which once served as a chapel but was later converted for use as a prison.

As we have seen elsewhere, an eighteenth-century park is not such a strange place to go in search of medieval England, since abbey ruins became prized attractions in the grounds of country houses as visual appetisers to enliven the view and endow it with poetic content. However, at **Stourhead** Henry Hoare's quest for the Picturesque extended to the importation of authentic relics of the Middle Ages. When the city fathers of Bristol decided that their city's High Cross stood in the way of progress, it was dismantled in 1762 and then sold to Henry Hoare. In 1765 it was unpacked and re-assembled at Stourhead, where it has been well cared for ever since. Although the structure has been restored several times and its present context of a country park is hopelessly wrong, the **Bristol High Cross** still conveys a powerful impression of the effect these magnificent Gothic monuments once created as the focal point of England's towns and cities.

After a brief stop at **Old Wardour Castle** where some Renaissance flourishes were added to the medieval castle before it, too, became no more than an object of antique curiosity in

CHURCH STYLES. *The Dorset town of Abbotsbury provides contrasting examples of ecclesiastical design: the familiar shape of the parish church* (left) *and the heavily buttressed St Catherine's Chapel* (above) *on a nearby hill resembling a miniature castle.*

the landscaped park of a Palladian country house, we catch up once more with Alfred the Great at **Shaftesbury**. We have it on the reliable authority of William of Malmesbury, quoting a now vanished inscription from the chapter house of the abbey, that in the year 880 'Alfred made this town'. In fact, Shaftesbury served as Alfred's provisional capital before the royal throne of Wessex was removed to Winchester. Shaftesbury was thus a highly significant halt along the road to the consolidation of Saxon power. In 888 Alfred founded here a Benedictine abbey for women. The thirteenth-century paraphrase of Alfred's deed of foundation records: 'I King Alfred, do give and grant in honour of God, the Virgin Mary and All Saints for the health of my soul, to the Church of Shaftesbury, one hundred hides of land.' This was an honest admission of self-interest, for the founders of monasteries were all most concerned with the health of their souls.

Alas, the extant remains of this royal nunnery are scant indeed; and there is nothing of Alfredian date to excite the antiquarian. **Shaftesbury Abbey** was entirely rebuilt by the Normans between 1080 and 1120, the funds deriving from the donations of pilgrims to the shrine of St Edward, King and Martyr. This now half-forgotten Saxon King of England had been brutally murdered by his half-brother Aethelred in 978 at Corfe in Dorset and buried at Wareham; but on account of the Danish raids the body was transferred for safety to the hilltop 'burh' of Shaftesbury and interred amidst great ceremony in the abbey church. Perhaps the nuns of Shaftesbury had an eye to the main chance, because the tragic fate of the king elevated him to the status of martyr; and there were reports of miraculous cures occasioned by his holy relics even while they were still lodged at Wareham. In due course Edward was canonised, and the already well endowed Shaftesbury Abbey found itself even better off as one of the great pilgrimage centres that would be emulated in later centuries by Canterbury with Thomas Becket and Gloucester with another royal and martyred Edward.

Excavations at Shaftesbury in 1931 uncovered a roughly made lead casket full of bones from the skeleton of a youth showing injuries commensurate with a violent death. These have been generally accepted as the true relics of St Edward, but the final resting place of the saintly bones has yet to be decided. The excavator lodged them in a bank vault for many years and then in 1988 presented them to a Russian Orthodox Church in Surrey. Meanwhile, there has been legal action to bring about the return of the bones to their proper home in Shaftesbury. For the time being, Shaftesbury Abbey has an empty lead casket.

From Shaftesbury to Sherborne is but a short hop westward along the A30 which straddles the borderline of Dorset and Wiltshire, but a slight detour takes in **Fiddleford Manor**, one mile east of Sturminster Newton. This uninhabited house possesses a medieval open timber roof much acclaimed by architectural historians as a textbook illustration of cusped arch-braced trusses, purlins and massive beams, all held together entirely by wooden pegs. Only necessary restoration has been undertaken and the new timber is easily distinguishable from the smoke-blackened original, but that does not impair the appreciation of this delightful manorial residence.

The town of **Sherborne** presents itself today as a quiet backwater whose main activity centres around the famous school, but this was from earliest times an ecclesiastical town of the utmost importance. In the year 705 St Aldhelm became the first Bishop of Sherborne and built his cathedral probably to the west of the present **Sherborne Abbey**. This foundation marked the westward expansion of Saxon Christianity; and Sherborne was to remain the seat of the bishopric covering the West Country until 909. At the height of its fortunes it ministered unto a see comprising the whole of Dorset, Somerset, Devon and Cornwall, until its territory was subdivided with the establishment of Wells and Crediton. The only physical evidence of Saxon Sherborne is a blocked doorway in the west wall of the abbey church, but this dates back only to the last of several rebuildings prior to the Norman Conquest, carried out in around 1050 by Bishop Alfwold.

As if to deny its ancient lineage Sherborne Abbey is now dressed up in the garb of the Perpendicular, the last phase of Gothic. Having lost its cathedral status in 1075 Sherborne continued to flourish as a Benedictine abbey. The monks resolved in the middle of the fifteenth century to rebuild their old Norman church in the most lavish fashion of the day: their fan-vaulted nave and choir stood in the avant-garde of architectural daring at the time. But not all was sweetness and light and to the greater glory of God, for a bitter quarrel had been simmering between the monks and the townsfolk over access to the baptismal font.

Matters came to a head in 1437 when, in the course of a violent protest against the monks' obstructive attitude, 'one Walter Gallor, a stoute bocher, dwelling yn Shirburn, defacid clene the fonte-stone'. Uproar ensued and a riot broke out. In the passion of the moment, as John Leland's account continues, 'a preste of Al-Hawlois shot a shaft with fier into the toppe of that part of S Marye chirch that devidid the est part that the monkes usid from the townes-men usid: and this partition chauncing at that tyme to be thakkid yn, the rofe was sette a fier, and consequently al the hole chirch, the lede and belles meltid, was defacid.' As a punishment the townsfolk were obliged to contribute their labour to the rebuilding of the abbey church, but the situation eventually resolved itself in their favour at the Dissolution when they acquired Sherborne Abbey for their own parochial use. Nothing is known of the fate of the pyromaniac priest, but the burnt scars caused by the conflagration can still be seen on the masonry.

Sherborne's medieval past lurks also in the ruins of its **Old Castle**, a Norman foundation acquired by Sir Walter Raleigh in 1592. This Renaissance gentleman actually tried to convert the ancient pile into a contemporary residence, but he soon abandoned the attempt and by 1594 he had installed himself in a lodge which now forms part of a country house that has usurped the name of Sherborne Castle.

There is a unique medieval phenomenon to be seen in the parish church of the Dorset village of **Whitchurch Canonicorum**. In the north transept is the Shrine of St Candida (originally St Wite): a tomb chest with three round openings for pilgrims to touch the coffin containing the bones of a lady of small stature. This is the only instance in England of a

THE MERCHANT OF SOUTHAMPTON. *The restoration by English Heritage of the wine merchant's premises in French Street gives a vivid impression of medieval commerce and its attendant domestic lifestyle.*

A WORLD OF COLOUR AND COMFORT. *Gaily painted furniture, a generous hearth, a ceiling of oak and a floor of beaten earth combine to create a cosy and reassuring environment within.*

parish church still possessing the actual shrine of the saint who figures in its dedication. People still place their petitions and votive offerings here, the latest in an unbroken chain of supplicants reaching back into the most distant reaches of the Middle Ages. St Candida still enjoys a particular reputation for the healing of ailments affecting the eyes.

At **Abbotsbury**, on the Dorset coast overlooking the western end of Chesil Beach, the Middle Ages might seem hardly to have ended at all. The famous Swannery goes back at least to 1393 when first reference to it is found. Thatching reeds are still cultivated in the neighbourhood and stored in the roofed half of a magnificent tithe barn built by the Benedictines in the early fifteenth century. Nothing much is to be seen of the abbey, but the parish church is a gem; and a walk to the top of a nearby hill brings into focus one of the most curious of religious buildings. The heavily buttressed **St Catherine's Chapel** has a solid, fortified appearance; and the interior has a tunnel vault of stone, to which the closest parallels are to be sought in Scotland rather than the south of England. The commanding views over the pebble beach and out to sea suggest a watchtower or a lighthouse. There has been so little modern development in Abbotsbury that the ghosts of the Middle Ages still walk the streets, in a manner of speaking.

Elsewhere in Dorset the medieval spirit is alive and well. **Athelhampton House** is a gorgeous manor of the late Middle Ages. The unfinished but glorious **Milton Abbey** appears detached from the twentieth century. The church at **Bere Regis** boasts a painted timber roof, resplendent with life-sized, carved figures of the Apostles. **Wareham**, another of Alfred's 'burhs' has important Saxon fabric in its two ancient churches. But in this part of Dorset all roads lead to that strategic gap in the Purbeck Hills guarded by the ruins of **Corfe Castle**, which was efficiently slighted after the Civil War in the seventeenth century so that its surviving piles of masonry are all akimbo as if from an earth tremor. Further south on a remote headland stands the square **St Aldhelm's Chapel**, an enigmatic Norman structure dedicated to a Saxon saint.

We now approach **Southampton**, one of the great commercial cities of medieval England, which, after years of neglect, is reasserting its proud urban past. English Heritage has not only restored the premises of a medieval wine merchant at 58 French Street, but has refurnished them with modern reproductions of the sort of chairs, tables, beds and cupboards that would have graced these rooms in the fourteenth century. As the name French Street suggests, this part of Southampton was probably settled by colonists from Normandy around the time of the Conquest and was engaged in trade with France at a very early date. The house was originally built in around 1290 by John Fortin, whose main business was the wine trade with Bordeaux. The half-timbered dwelling sits over a stone-vaulted cellar used for the storage of wine which was sold directly over the counter at the front of the house. The ground floor was – and is still – composed of nothing more sophisticated than beaten earth strewn with rushes or straw. The rooms of the first floor are open to the rafters, making them difficult to heat in winter but delightfully airy in summer.

The scarred ruins of Corfe Castle, Dorset.

The hall may be modest by baronial standards, but it rises the full height of the building and occupies one third of the entire accommodation. It provided a prestigious setting for entertaining guests, who would doubtless have been invited to sample their host's extensive wine list. This is a wonderful place to recapture the atmosphere of the family trading-houses that were characteristic of the Middle Ages. Transactions were concluded with the soft clink of silver on an oak board or by the scratch of a quill on parchment.

It is worth extracting every ounce of medieval memories from this small house in French Street before embarking on the search for Southampton's other relics of the Middle Ages which have to contend with all the busy apparatus of a modern city. But there are some impressive sights, such as the majestic **Bargate** guarding the northern entrance to the city, and the atmospheric group of buildings at **West Gate**. The ancient parish church of **St Michael** – named after the patron saint of Normandy – still surveys the much changed urban

BUILT TO IMPRESS. *The richly emblazoned and heavily defensive Bargate of Southampton was designed both as a status symbol and as a deterrent to aggressors.*

A MEDIEVAL FAKE. *The authenticity of Arthur's Round Table in the Great Hall of Winchester Castle is no longer in dispute. It was made not in Arthurian times but during the late thirteenth century. The painting dates from the Tudor period.*

scene, although its sturdy Norman tower is now surmounted by a graceful eighteenth-century spire. A late fourteenth wool warehouse still stands in Bugle Street; and archaeologists are revealing the vaults and foundations of many medieval houses at the lower end of the High Street. Examination of the domestic refuse of Richard of Southwick's house of the late thirteenth century has shown an amazingly rich and varied lifestyle, of which some of the ingredients were ceramics from France and Spain, Persian silk, Venetian glass and an exotic array of imported wines and comestibles to supplement the native produce. Like Bristol and Exeter, those other great trading cities in the region, Southampton depended mainly on its buoyant export of woollen cloth to finance its cosmopolitan import bill.

Today Southampton is a vibrant commercial port while Winchester is a stately, ecclesiastical city, but in the Middle Ages the latter was no slumbering cathedral town but an equally vibrant centre, animated by cloth manufacture and its attendant commerce. The way to Winchester can be agreeably lengthened by a southerly detour to take in the ruined abbeys of **Netley** and **Titchfield** as well as **Portchester Castle**, where a Norman keep and a priory church were raised within the confines of the old Roman fort. Heading north, at **Bishop's Waltham** we come across an outpost of the fabulously wealthy Henry of Blois, a prince as well as Bishop of Winchester from 1129 to 1171 and Abbot of Glastonbury. This was a country palace which stood in a park of some 10,000 acres. Another, and more imposing palace of Bishop Henry of Blois may be found at Winchester in the ruins of **Wolvesey Palace**, one quarter of a mile south-east of the cathedral. But the enormous outlay on palatial accommodation was not the limit of this clerical magnate's building ambitions; for he also endowed the **Hospital of the Holy Cross** near by. Under its more popular name of St Cross this establishment became one of England's best-known almshouses.

Bishop Henry contributed much to the prosperity of **Winchester** and revived the city from the relative decline which set in as it became increasingly ignored by the kings of England from Henry I onward. The destruction by fire of the old royal palace in 1141 effectively ended Winchester's pretensions even as an occasional ceremonial capital: in fact, Bishop Henry used material from the ruins for his own palace at Wolvesey. At this time Winchester imposed its economic strength as the largest town in the region with an extremely diverse commercial activity, of which the highlight was the annual fair on St Giles's Hill to the east of the city. This was without doubt the most important medieval trade fair in the southern half of England and one of the great events of the year. It was held under the authority of the Bishop of Winchester; and the revenues from its tolls substantially boosted the income already pouring into the episcopal coffers. It lasted for more than two weeks and was attended by traders from all over Europe as well as England herself.

Although the economic pre-eminence of medieval Winchester is thus beyond doubt, our present perception of the city is based on its two major monuments of the period: the Great Hall of the castle and the cathedral. Winchester Castle was begun by William the Conqueror at the very beginning of 1067 and sixty houses were demolished to make way for it. As the

Bishop's Waltham Palace in Hampshire.

VICTIM OF THE DISSOLUTION. *The roofless nave and choir of Netley Abbey, Hampshire, provide eloquent testimonials to the enormous loss in superb ecclesiastical architecture following Henry VIII's suppression of the monasteries.*

THE BEAUTY OF THE VAULT. *The spreading web of the mighty Gothic vault in the nave of Winchester Cathedral is alive with strength and lines of tension. Yet it has all the serenity of a work of art.*

capital of Saxon England and as the city of Alfred the Great, Winchester had enormous symbolic significance. The castle grew at the expense of the old Saxon royal palace, but soon ceased to be a regular seat of royalty. Nevertheless it remained the repository of the Treasury, the Exchequer and the Domesday Book until the late twelfth century. Henry III was born in Winchester in 1206 and he did much to restore the prestige of his native city by spending generously on the castle and building between 1222 and 1235 the **Great Hall**. This has been acclaimed as 'the finest surviving aisled hall of the thirteenth century'; and indeed it is the only surviving part of the entire castle since the rest was demolished on the orders of Oliver Cromwell.

Interest in the Great Hall focuses on the huge, 18-foot in diameter Round Table suspended on the west wall, resembling – as some disrespectful wit aptly quipped – a gigantic dart board. It is only recently that scientific analysis has enabled an accurate dating of the table top to the second half of the thirteenth century. It was most probably commissioned by Edward I who reigned from 1272 to 1307, for this monarch's other Arthurian activities included the opening of the supposed tombs of Arthur and Guinevere in 1278 at Glastonbury Abbey. The Winchester Round Table was originally supported by twelve stout legs around its circumference and a huge block at its centre. The painting of Arthur holding sword and orb dates only from the early sixteenth century, as can be roughly deduced from the huge Tudor Rose in the middle. The Tudor family of Welsh origin was naturally keen to establish a link with Arthur as a remote and illustrious example of Celtic kingship. From our present perspective it is fascinating to observe how the Arthurian legend resurfaces over the centuries, firstly in the age of chivalry in the thirteenth century as an ideal of knighthood, then in the sixteenth century as a political parable, and finally in the nineteenth century as a romantic legend of a lost world. The possibilities for history to feed off itself seem endless.

But the Great Hall with its Round Table is really but a sideshow next to **Winchester Cathedral** which ranks as the longest Gothic church in the whole of Europe. It was conceived on a scale commensurate with its illustrious past as the burial place of Saxon kings, including of course Alfred the Great. The Norman nave was remodelled in the new Perpendicular style in the closing decades of the fourteenth century, but the transepts have retained their original character and are a very rare example of Norman work dating right back to the time of the Conqueror. Sadly, there is nothing visible to give us an idea of Bishop Aethelwold's cathedral of the late tenth century when Winchester was at the summit of its fortunes as capital of England. However, the Early English retro-choir contains the largest expanse of medieval floortiles in the country. This is an interior packed with architectural interest although the exterior gives little hint of it.

Salisbury Cathedral offers a totally different experience as the purest large-scale essay in Early English Gothic. The unity of style comes from the fact that it was built in just forty years from its foundation in 1220, although the steeple was a later addition. The reason for this comparatively late date is that the town of **Salisbury** itself was actually a new town, the most successful of many in the Middle Ages. It was laid out on a grid pattern, divided into regular plots or 'chequers' by the intersecting streets. It occupied a well watered and convenient site and immediately grew prosperous as a centre of cloth manufacture, aided by the proximity of the sheep-grazing lands of Salisbury Plain. Commercial rivalry between town and cathedral led to the construction of a solid wall around the Close and the imposing High Street Gate of 1327. Although Salisbury has been subject to constant rebuilding, the basic layout of the 'chequers' has withstood the pressures of redevelopment. Some fine, old houses have survived, most notably that of the wool merchant John a Port in Queen Street of about 1450; and behind the incongruous façade of a cinema in New Canal lurks the totally unexpected late fifteenth-century interior of the house of John Halle, another wealthy wool merchant.

The reason for this outstanding foundation of a medieval new town at Salisbury is not far to seek. Just two miles north of the city lies the now abandoned Iron Age hillfort of **Old Sarum**, which by a quirk of history remained a centre of human settlement well into the Middle Ages and continued, long after it had lost all its inhabitants, to return a Member of Parliament to Westminster, for this was the most notorious of the 'rotten boroughs' abolished by the Great Reform Act of 1832. In the early Middle Ages, however, Old Sarum was a flourishing concern. The Council of London of 1075 ordered the transfer of the see of Sherborne to Old Sarum ostensibly on the grounds that it was a more populous place; but it is not at all certain that this was so, for Old Sarum consisted chiefly of a castle, which was later rebuilt by Bishop Roger at the beginning of the twelfth century. These are the scant ruins to be encountered today; but more significant are the outlines in the grass of the predecessors of Salisbury Cathedral, whose stone was later plundered to build the wall around the Close in Salisbury.

The roots of Old Sarum's abandonment lay in the bitter animosity which developed between the cathedral clergy and the castle garrison and erupted into an open feud. After years of unhappy co-existence, the clergy were eventually successful in lobbying the Pope for permission to transfer the cathedral to a fresh site at New Sarum, now known as Salisbury. Among the litany of complaints about Old Sarum listed by the clergy was the whiteness of the chalk landscape which they alleged was the cause of blindness. Old Sarum has been left to its own devices for several centuries, and its first role, that of the hillfort, has re-asserted itself. The whole complex now has that distinctive quality of an ancient monument; and it is truly difficult to imagine a cathedral, castle and township all sharing this windswept summit in Wiltshire. Nowhere are the Middle Ages more elusive than here.

One of the mythical founders of Bristol, on St John's Gate.

IX. WEST COUNTRY

HE PRE-EMINENCE OF **Bristol** in the Middle Ages may be measured from the fact that in 1373 the city was granted separate status as a metropolitan county in its own right. Its strategic location as a port wedged in between the wool-producing areas of Somerset and Gloucestershire made the early fortunes of Bristol's merchants. The wine trade with the Gascon vintners of the Bordeaux region also has ancient roots and contributed much to Bristol's emergence as a prosperous medieval city with a mighty castle, a rich Augustinian abbey, a noble bridge with shops and houses just like the one in London, and a labyrinth of tight, twisting streets crammed with dwellings, huddled along the river banks at the confluence of the Avon and the Frome. From here, Bristol's lifeline of water extended down to the Severn and into the Bristol Channel like a silver highway, providing convenient access to the ports of Europe's western seaboard and to America as well, for it was from Bristol that in 1497 John Cabot set sail for the New World.

Alas, first impressions of Bristol today convey little of the atmosphere of its proud medieval past. The castle is no more than a few bumps in the grass of a municipal park; the once famous Bristol Bridge is now a provisional affair of recent date; and the urban landscape has been redeveloped and blitzed in the course of the centuries. The abbey remains, rescued by its elevation as **Bristol Cathedral** at the Dissolution, but it stands somewhat apart from the ancient city centre, decidedly marginal in comparison to the cathedrals of York, Lincoln or Canterbury which are the heart and soul of their cities. Yet something of the Middle Ages lingers on in the narrow, meandering street pattern of the old town; and one gradually becomes aware, amid the modern buildings, of a silent host of redundant medieval churches sticking up like so many tombstones of vanished communities, to indicate the position of parishes which once spilled over with human life.

The ruined shell of St Mary-le-Port rises wraith-like behind the offices of an insurance company; beyond in Castle Park the empty carcass of St Peter's has none of the charm of an artful Gothic ruin, but looks abandoned in every respect. The **Temple Church** with its leaning tower has at least been accorded the dignified status of an ancient monument. Elsewhere, the picture is brighter: the church of **St Nicholas** at the northern end of Bristol

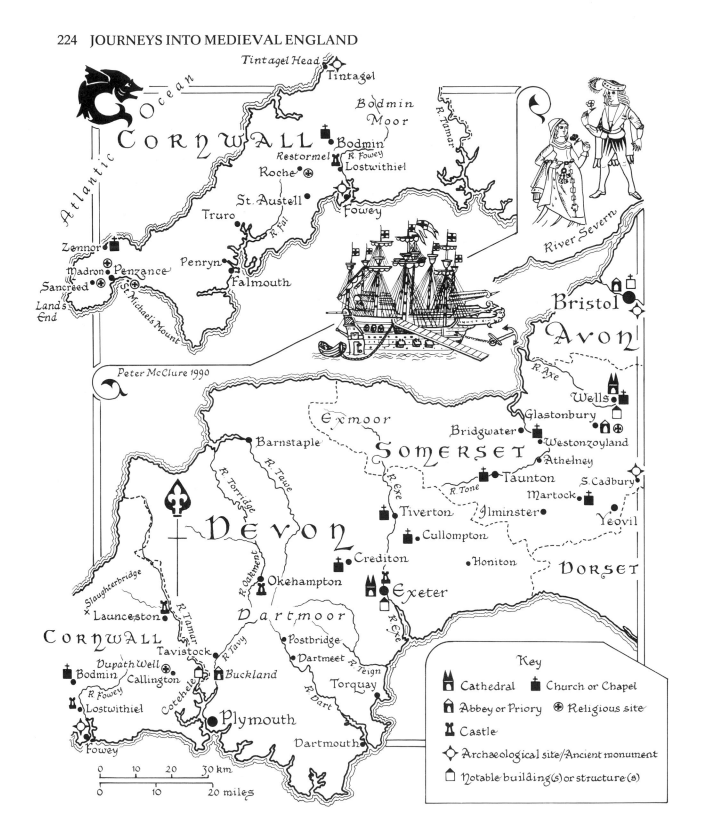

Atlantic Ocean

Tintagel Head

Tintagel

Bodmin Moor

CORNWALL

Bodmin
Restormel · R. Fowey
Roche · Lostwithiel
St. Austell
Truro · Fowey
R. Fal
Zennor
Penryn
Madron · Penzance
Sancreed · Falmouth
Land's End · St. Michael's Mount

R. Tamar

River Severn

Bristol
Avon

R. Axe

Wells

Glastonbury
Bridgwater · Westonzoyland
SOMERSET · Athelney
R. Exe · Taunton · S. Cadbury
R. Tone · Martock
Barnstaple · Tiverton · Ilminster · Yeovil
R. Torridge · R. Tawe · Cullompton
Exmoor · Honiton
DORSET
Peter McClure 1990

DEVON

Crediton
R. Oakment
Okehampton
Dartmoor · Exeter
R. Teign
Slaughterbridge
Launceston · R. Tamar · Postbridge
CORNWALL · Dartmeet
Tavistock · R. Tavy · R. Dart
Dupath Well · Buckland · Torquay
Bodmin · Callington · Cotehele
R. Fowey · Plymouth
Lostwithiel
Fowey · Dartmouth

0   10   20   30 km
0   10   20 miles

Key

Cathedral   Church or Chapel

Abbey or Priory   Religious site

Castle

Archaeological site/Ancient monument

Notable building(s) or structure(s)

Bridge has been put to excellent use as a museum of Bristol's urban history, and at the top of Broad Street there is the charming sight of **St John the Baptist**, as a church redundant but still lovingly maintained. The building extends over the last remaining of the gates of Bristol where two medieval carved figures, representing the mythical founders of Bristol, Brennus and Bellinus, watch over the arch. Recently repainted in what might have been their original colours, they provide a vivid reminder of the visual richness of townscapes in the Middle Ages. A coat of arms shows a merchant ship under sail and the now vanished castle: the twin emblems of medieval Bristol.

The roll call of Bristol's ancient churches could continue with **St James's**, marooned between the coach station and the new Broadmead shopping centre which conceals behind its concrete modernity the surprising remains of the city's Dominican friary complete with a hall under a roof of fourteenth-century oak beams. But pride of place goes without doubt to the still thriving parish church of **St Mary Redcliffe**, now virtually stranded on a traffic island ensnared by Bristol's urban expressways. This church, described by Queen Elizabeth I as 'the fairest, goodliest and most famous parish church in England', was completed through the munificence of the Bristolian merchant William Canynges who died in 1474. His effigy lies inside the church in quasi-regal splendour. But much of Bristol's medieval heritage lies underground, hidden from sight, such as the ancient cellars in Denmark Street, once owned by the Augustinians and still in use by John Harvey and Sons Limited for storing port and sherry.

By complete contrast to Bristol, the ancient city of **Wells** has retained for all to see at first glance the essential components of a compact medieval city whose face has not been re-arranged out of all recognition. Indeed, the approach from the south-east leads across an open space, a combination of field and parkland, which has never been built on. This affords a noble vista of the cathedral rising up from behind the massive, protecting wall of the Bishop's Palace, whose moat is fed from those natural wells commemorated in the name of the city. This is a view, not overshadowed by blocks of flats or offices, that would still be recognisable to the citizens of Wells back in the fifteenth century when the cathedral received its last architectural flourish with the final Perpendicular stage of the tower, whose great weight is supported by those mighty scissor arches dominating the nave.

The earliest parts of the **Bishop's Palace** in Wells go back to the 1230s and were built by the same masons employed on the west front of the cathedral with its splendid sculpture gallery. Bishop Jocelin's hall, dating from the thirteenth century, is still there within the palace, although subdivided into smaller rooms. Ralph of Shrewsbury, Bishop of Wells from 1329 to 1363, was the incumbent responsible for the circuit wall and moat. There was of course an element of prestige and showmanship in such a fortification, but security was as much a concern of clerics and prelates as of squires and magnates during the Middle Ages.

Bishop Ralph was the inspiration behind another great building initiative of medieval Wells. Just to the north of the cathedral, and entered through an archway, there is a cobbled

TOWERS OF DELIGHT. *The art of building majestic church towers reached its height in the county of Somerset. In this fine example at Westonzoyland the successive stages are finally crowned by elegant tracery.*

THE BISHOP'S DEFENCE. *This stout bastion and broad moat were not the work of king or baron but of a cleric. The Bishop of Wells saw fit to protect in this way his episcopal palace. Wells Cathedral can be seen behind the ramparts.*

The angel roof in the church of St Cuthbert, Wells.

street flanked by terraces of houses on either side culminating in a comely chapel. This truly magnificent piece of medieval urbanism was inaugurated by Bishop Ralph in the 1340s in order to form a closed community for the vicars who represented the canons at the cathedral services eight times a day, between them having to work their way through the entire psalter of 150 psalms. Such a strenuous routine was evidently not enough in itself to absorb the full energies of the vicars who, living in various lodgings among the townsfolk, fell easy prey to the temptations of urban life. Drinking, gambling and fornication provided relief for some vicars from the discipline and tedium of the daily round. Thus Bishop Ralph's idea, as realised in the **Vicars' Close**, was to enclose the vicars within a college-like environment and thereby shield them physically from the temptations of the secular domain. This was also the guiding light behind the contrivance known as the Chain Gate, added in 1459, which facilitated the passage of the vicars via a bridge directly from the cathedral to their close without allowing them to set foot on the ground. To many a reluctant vicar this must have been a veritable 'bridge of sighs', affording a brief glimpse of the outside world as they passed from one closed environment to another.

Much time can be passed in and around the cathedral, Bishop's Palace and the Wells Liberty, as that part of the city originally developed by the cathedral is known. The area is still entered via gateways such as Penniless Porch and Brown's Gate, ornamental archways of the fifteenth century which demarcated fiscal and administrative frontiers. Within the town but outside the Liberty stands the parish church of **St Cuthbert**, whose exceptionally fine timber roof with its carved angels, shields and rosettes has been gloriously restored in recent years. St Cuthbert's may also serve as an introduction to the phenomenal collection of Perpendicular church towers, perhaps inspired by that of Wells Cathedral, with which the towns and villages of Somerset sought to glorify God during the fifteenth century when they were at the height of their material fortune.

Among a host of equally worthy examples, the church of **Westonzoyland** demonstrates the main features of the Somerset type. Its tower rises in four stages to a height of 100 feet, modest perhaps but within its flat, natural context of the Somerset Levels forming an imposing landmark. The wooden roof, swarming with angels, is one of the finest in the county, to be ranked alongside that of the renowned All Saints at Martock. The heavenly host appears to be almost physically present at Westonzoyland, fluttering high above the nave.

Near by is the village of **Athelney**, set in a terrain now efficiently drained but which was once a nigh impenetrable bogland where Alfred the Great took refuge from the Danes in 878 when his military fortunes were at their lowest ebb. There is no material relic of Alfred's enforced sojourn in the marshes of Athelney, and the landscape has changed beyond recognition, but this is nevertheless a locality which retains a significant historic value by virtue of its association with the launching of the Saxon counter-offensive. For without the dogged resistance and loyalty of the men of Somerset, the Saxon cause would have been utterly lost. Instead, Alfred was able to re-emerge from his obscure redoubt at Athelney and to re-establish a Saxon kingdom with successive capitals at Shaftesbury and Winchester as the tide of war turned steadily in his favour.

The most majestic of the Somerset collection of church towers awaits at the church of **St Mary Magdalene, Taunton**. This intricate structure of golden Ham Hill stone interlaced with Quantock red sandstone is adorned with crocketed pinnacles at each of its four stages which rise to a crown of pierced battlements some 163 feet above the ground. Truly inspirational both in conception and execution, this tower was striking enough to impress the Georgian city planners who laid out Hammett Street: for this thoroughfare of Classical frontages is aligned on the medieval church tower as if in homage.

As we cross into Devon there are other kinds of ecclesiastical beauty in store, but the art of the church tower may be considered to have reached its zenith in Somerset. At **Tiverton**, the church of **St Peter** possesses one of the most spectacular of chantry chapels to be added to a parish church. It was endowed in 1517 by John Greenway, a successful merchant of the City of London as well as of Tiverton. The chief interest of this structure of dazzling white stone lies in the sculptural decoration of its exterior. Here we see portrayed in picture-book fashion a flotilla of merchant vessels, some armed with cannon, sailing the high seas with their export cargoes of woollen cloth and imports of wines and spices, a highly lucrative trade which enabled John Greenway to perform this very public act of religious devotion. The masons have carved all manner of nautical detail, which makes these stone illustrations of late medieval sailing craft invaluable references to the naval historian. Perhaps out of rivalry John Lane endowed a magnificent fan-vaulted aisle added to the church of **St Andrew, Cullompton**. Greenway and Lane were thus the Devonian counterparts of the wealthy clothiers of East Anglia who left their mark on the wool churches of that region.

On the face of it, the **Church of the Holy Cross** in **Crediton** might appear to belong to the

MERCHANTS BID FOR PARADISE. *John Greenway of Tiverton endowed his parish church with a dazzling chantry chapel of white stone (above). His rival John Lane at Cullompton responded with a new aisle where clothiers are carved on the columns (right).*

same category, for its stately Perpendicular exterior also belongs to the late Middle Ages when the great rebuilding of England's parish churches took place. But this elegant fabric conceals a foundation of immense antiquity going back to early Saxon times which owes its existence most probably to the intervention of St Boniface, the evangeliser of several Germanic kingdoms who began life in Crediton under the name of Winfrith. A monastery was founded at Crediton in the year 739 shortly after St Boniface's visit to the Pope in Rome. In 909 Crediton was made a cathedral, a status it retained until 1050 when the bishopric was transferred to Exeter. It remained an important church nevertheless, and it displays significant portions of Norman work dating back to around 1150. Its name is now linked to that of Exeter, in that there is a Bishop of Crediton appointed as suffragan to the Bishop of Exeter; and it is in that city that the Bishop of Crediton is now to be found.

The main east-west route through Devon passes through **Exeter**, which since the establishment of a legionary fortress – then known as Isca Dumnoniorum – has made steady progress as an urban centre. John Leland noted in the 1530s that the city was 'right strongly waullid and maintenid'; and indeed, some impressive stretches of medieval wall on Roman foundations have survived, albeit not on the scale of York or Chester. The essential layout of the inner city still follows the rectilinear orientation of the Roman settlement which came through the Middle Ages virtually unchanged in the alignment of Fore Street, High Street, North Street and South Street. The northern corner of the city within the walls was occupied by **Rougemont Castle**. This was a most important bastion of Norman power in the south-west, built as early as 1068 when William the Conqueror visited Exeter in person in pursuit of his bloody suppression of the Western Rebellions. A huge chunk of the city was razed to the ground to clear a site for the castle and some forty-eight houses were demolished. The most telling survival at Rougemont is the powerful gatehouse, a fascinating structure, since it bears some characteristic Saxon features such as the triangular-headed windows. We must imagine that the subjugated Saxons were drafted as forced labour on the project. In those early years after the Conquest the need to build quickly prevailed over any question of style. If masons trained in the Norman tradition were unavailable, then the Saxons would have to be allowed to build as best they could. However, once Norman civilisation was firmly established, no such stylistic aberrations were to be tolerated. Rougemont Castle thus represents a very brief turning point in history when one culture was replacing another. The interior of the castle is today occupied by post-medieval buildings which are used by the local assizes.

As for the town itself, the **Guildhall** has a venerable medieval ancestry reaching back to 1160. The fabric of the hall can fairly be dated to around 1330, but it subsequently underwent considerable remodelling. Its present oak roof is a 1468 replacement of the original, and the extravagant portico, such a bold feature of the High Street, was an Elizabethan addition in the 1590s. This hybrid architectural composition has weathered the storms of the centuries to claim the title of the oldest functioning municipal premises in the country. The less conspicuous Hall of the Weavers, Fullers and Shearmen of 1471, known simply as the **Tuckers' Hall**, serves as a reminder that medieval Exeter's fortunes were based, as were those of most other cities, on the wool and cloth trade.

The pride of the city, then as now, was **Exeter Cathedral**, which developed from a Norman core into what has been praised as England's finest large-scale display of Decorated Gothic. Its highlights are the statue-covered west front, which like that at Wells would once have been a riot of colour, and the 300-foot-long continuous vault extending without interruption from west to east to form the longest unbroken stretch of Gothic vaulting.

The west front of Exeter Cathedral.

Take note also of the Bishop's Throne of 1312, rising in emulation of a church spire, but carved in Devon oak in a crescendo of intricate carpentry to a height of almost sixty feet. This throne is more of a miniature building than a piece of furniture and serves to underline the enormous social rank and prestige attaching to a bishop during the Middle Ages.

Despite such magnificent artifice, one of the most gripping experiences of medieval Exeter is to be found in the subterranean conduits beneath the city, known rather prosaically as the **Underground Passages**. A discreet entrance in the modern shopping precinct leads down into a maze of tunnels carved out of the rock on which Exeter stands. They are probably of medieval origin, although some would have them going back to Roman times. It seems that they were created to provide an efficient water-distribution system. Stories abound of their use as secret passages out of the city, but this would have been secondary to their function as a civic amenity.

Beyond Exeter to the west, the vast upland expanse of Dartmoor has long resisted attempts at human settlement. As the numerous prehistoric remains inform us, the climate of the Bronze Age was much more favourable to agriculture than that of today; and in the

A MEDIEVAL SCULPTURE GALLERY. *This was the bold concept for the entire west front of Exeter Cathedral. Originally, the statues would have been painted in bright colours to create an overwhelming effect.*

A FOREST CARVED IN STONE. *The nave vault of Exeter Cathedral has been likened to an avenue of trees whose branches reach out and flow into one another. A spectacular vision of those medieval masons.*

Middle Ages there occurred another window of opportunity for mankind to eke some sort of living from the moor. Flushed with the optimism of the pioneer, the settlers at **Hound Tor** must have been justifiably proud of their taming of virgin territory, but their hamlet was doomed as the climate gradually deteriorated during the late thirteenth century. By the beginning of the fourteenth century this tiny huddle of stone hovels and a modest 'manor house' was deserted. No one has lived here since, and the grass-covered foundations are silent but for the sounds of nature, mostly the wind whistling across the granite outcrops.

The medieval attitude to Dartmoor was heavily tinged with fear and foreboding. Myths and legends came out of the swirling mists and driving rain which so often masked the scant trace of the tracks and bridleways. The prehistoric stones were embodiments of evil spirits, much to be feared in an age of superstition. By and large, Dartmoor was a sinister place to be crossed just as quickly as possible. The ancient clapper bridges such as that at **Dartmeet** and the better preserved example at **Postbridge** were built to aid the passage of packhorse traffic; and they would have been greeted with relief by medieval travellers as confirmation of another leg of the arduous journey successfully completed as well as reassurance that they were on the right track.

Once the rigours of Dartmoor have been safely endured, a land of gentler contours and richer promise along the valley of the River Tavy opens up. The river begins as a babbling brook on the western rim of Dartmoor and gathers force as it flows through **Tavistock**. Here once stood a Benedictine monastery of tremendous wealth, but there remain only scattered fragments to tell the tale. Further downstream, and in a better state of preservation, the old Cistercian house of **Buckland Abbey** presents a fascinating example of the conversion of monastic buildings into a country residence fit for a Tudor gentleman. In this case the client was the old seadog Sir Richard Grenville, who purchased the property from the Crown in 1539. It was later acquired by that other buccaneer Sir Francis Drake and subsequently handed down through many generations of the Drake family. Like all conversions, the old bits can never quite be reconciled with the new, and we can enjoy the awkward but pleasing spectacle of Tudor panelling and plaster ceilings within a framework of Gothic vaulting. A walk through Buckland Abbey offers swiftly alternating insights into the minds of the Cistercian monks and of Grenville and Drake, as two very different worlds are forced into juxtaposition. There is the lingering suspicion that the older structure might still yet be capable of rejecting the alien body which has been implanted, but all has been quiet these past 450 years.

The next great river valley to the west, that of the Tamar, divides Cornwall from the rest of England. Here, at a wooded spot on a bend in the river stands one of the most precious of late medieval houses in England. **Cotehele**, the name meaning simply 'wood by the estuary', was largely built by Sir Richard Edgcumbe who made the courageous decision to challenge Richard III over the suspected murder of the sons of Edward IV, those unfortunate 'Princes in the Tower'. Sir Richard Edgcumbe was hunted down at Cotehele by the King's agents and he fled the house with horsemen in hot pursuit. His line of escape was blocked by the Tamar, but he tried a last ruse by throwing his cap in the water to give the impression that he had drowned in an attempt to swim to safety. The trick succeeded, and his pursuers gave up the hunt. Sir Richard slipped away to France to join forces with Henry Tudor and fought alongside the future Henry VII at the Battle of Bosworth in 1485.

Sir Richard Edgcumbe celebrated the repossession of Cotehele by enlarging the old house, but its most impressive addition was the work of his son and heir Sir Piers Edgcumbe between 1489 and 1539. His greatest achievement was the Great Hall, one of the most

Bodmin Priory's famous Norman font.

atmospheric productions of the late Middle Ages. Much of what one sees at Cotehele has a charming homespun quality, built of rough but durable granite; and the house has been left remarkably unaltered but for the north-west tower, added in 1627.

As we proceed deeper into Cornwall we are confronted more and more with the myths and legends of the twilight years of the Celts, the roots of the Arthurian story and the early missionary work of the saints who travelled between Ireland, Wales and Brittany and worked so many miracles in this remote south-western tip of the British Isles long before the Saxons had accomplished their westward expansion. Here in Cornwall the concept of the Middle Ages must be stretched back firmly into the Dark Ages.

Not far from Callington lies **Dupath Well**, one of the most renowned of Cornwall's numerous holy wells. The existence of almost 200 is still known; and it is a guess just how many have disappeared or been lost from human memory. Like many others, Dupath acquired a stately well house in medieval times. The rivulet of clear water runs invitingly through the structure, comprising a tiny chapel which may once have contained an altar. The healing properties of individual wells are said to vary, and this one at Dupath enjoyed a

TALES OF THE DEEP. *Much of Cornish legend is born of the sea. The site of Arthur's mythical palace at Tintagel* (above) *is practically an island. A bench end at Zennor* (right) *commemorates a sad encounter between a mermaid and a local choirboy.*

reputation for the relief of whooping cough. The first edifice over the well, according to legend, was built by a knight Colan who died here after winning a duel for the hand of a maiden. This sad story is not a happy association for a holy well, but it is possible that an important element in the story has been lost somewhere along the line. The sanctity of the well is undoubtedly pre-Christian and considerably more ancient than its dedication to St Dominic would suggest.

At **Bodmin** we emerge from the spirit world of the Celts to admire in the church of **St Petroc** one of the most impressive of Norman fonts in the country, and probably the best known in Cornwall. The bowl of the font is truly massive, yet it appears at first glance to be supported entirely by the four slender columns adorned with angels at the corners. It rests, in fact, on a thick, solid central shaft. The symbolic presence of the angels, whose gazes together cover all points of the compass, is evidently to ward off any dark forces which may attempt to intrude on the holy sacrament of baptism. This spectacular composition reflects the stark confrontation of good and evil, the philosophical bedrock of medieval religious thought.

Restormel Castle takes us into the realm of medieval superpower politics, demonstrating that the Norman penetration of Cornwall was more efficient and aggressive than that of the Saxons. Architecturally, Restormel is a prime example of the shell-keep type of fortification; and its fortunes were closely linked to those of the nearby town of Lostwithiel, now a shadow of its former importance. It is a curious phenomenon that Norman castles in Cornwall still appear to be alien objects in the landscape, as indeed they were all over England, but here they have retained their capacity to surprise, as at Launceston where the castle really dominates its town from a lofty mound. So powerful yet in Cornwall is the Celtic identity of scattered hamlets and the more ancient megalithic monuments that the bastions of Norman power, even after nine hundred years or so, still obtrude in the most dramatic manner.

Just to the north of the seaport of Fowey stands a solitary monolith, known as the **Tristan Stone**, which takes us right back to the essence of things Cornish. The seven-foot stone bears a Latin inscription, which may be rendered as: 'Here lies Tristan, son of Cunomorus.' This Cunomorus was one of the sixth-century kings of Dumnonia who ruled over Cornwall and much of Devon; and the name is thought to be an alternative title for King Mark, the royal cuckold in the tragic love story of Tristan and Isolde, linked in time and place to the legendary figure of King Arthur. Sadly, it cannot be claimed that the stone marks Tristan's grave, for it was moved to its present location by the main road from its previous setting just to the south of the nearby Iron Age fortification of Castle Dore. As with most of the Arthurian relics in the West Country, the hard world of material fact only takes us a part of the way, leaving the imagination and a strong belief in legends to transport us to the heart of the myth.

St Michael's Mount also derives part of its potent appeal from elusive legendary associations. Its dramatic island situation, like that of Lindisfarne in Northumbria, is suspended twice daily by the receding tide when it may be reached on foot across the sands. This was the site of a monastery and a castle; now the rocky citadel is crowned by a romantic Victorian residence. St Michael's Mount figures in the legend of Tristan and Isolde as the patron or sponsor of the fair to which in the twelfth-century French version by Béroul, the hermit Ogrin came in order to buy garments and a horse for Isolde's reconciliation with King Mark. The Victorian architectural overlay at St Michael's Mount is perhaps too heavy, but the superb natural drama of this castle on its rocky island, especially when silhouetted against the setting sun, is enough on its own to support any number of myths and legends. Not surprisingly, its very name derives from a legend in which St Michael himself appeared to a hermit sitting on a rock by the seashore. Another version has St Michael manifest himself to a group of fishermen.

The Tristan Stone near Fowey offers a tenuous link with Arthurian legend.

The orthodox medievalist will find the Land's End peninsula too overwhelmed by the monuments of prehistory, but the Dark Ages are well represented by some magnificent Celtic crosses such as those at **Sancreed**; and at **Madron** there is another of those Cornish holy wells, this one with the remains of a tiny baptistery. Madron is still visited and venerated, as may be deduced from the many strips of cloth tied to the surrounding bushes and trees by those seeking relief from their suffering. In this exposed part of the country, the lowly churches of local granite appear to brace themselves against the prevailing winds off the Atlantic rather than reach for the sky like the noble towers of Somerset. But what they lack in sophistication, they make up for with their permanence, offering a solid, physical as well as spiritual shelter to those who enter.

Nowhere in Cornwall is the proximity of the sea to be forgotten. The rugged church at **Zennor** contains an exquisite wooden carving of a mermaid on a panel designed as a bench end. The legend attaching to this sensually rendered portrait is beautifully tragic. It seems

THE CHAPEL ON THE ROCK. *Built on a rugged granite outcrop at Roche in Cornwall is a fifteenth-century chapel marking the cave retreat of a Dark Age saint.*

THE GLORY THAT WAS GLASTONBURY. *The devastation of Glastonbury Abbey, one of the most prestigious and sacred of monastic sites in medieval England, marked in no uncertain terms the end of an era.*

that the mermaid was attracted by the heavenly singing of a chorister at Zennor and she lured him away to join her in her watery realm beneath the waves. The attractive likeness of the mermaid was carved on the orders of the boy's father in an attempt to flatter the fish-woman and tempt her out of the sea, and presumably to relinquish her captive in the process. As far as we know, the ruse failed; and the boy was never seen again, although some have claimed to hear his singing rising from the depths of the sea.

Such stories appear almost credible as long as you are in the grip of the mysterious primeval powers of Cornwall. All manner of visions are possible in this stark habitat which provides few distractions from the titanic clash of the elements. The wild, austere qualities of the landscape must have appealed to those visionary hermits of the early years of Christianity who sought spiritual light in their dark caves and shelters in Cornwall. At **Roche**, the cell of a Cornish hermit in a rocky outcrop was crowned in the fifteenth century by a tiny chapel which protrudes like a natural extension of the living rock. The original occupant of the cell is thought to have been St Gonand, a leper.

At **Tintagel** on the north coast of Cornwall, facing due west out across the Atlantic and braving its colossal impact, stands a rocky promontory, almost severed from the mainland by the sea. This place holds the key to the Arthurian legend, for this is the spot claimed as the birthplace of Arthur. The obvious visible remains are of a much later medieval castle, but archaeologists believed until recently that they had identified a fifth-century Celtic monastery as well. Scholarly opinion has now veered towards interpreting the remains in question as the outline of a princely household of roughly Arthurian date. Might this really have been Arthur's palace? If so, it must be said straight away that it was not the magnificent residence, as imagined by later purveyors of the legend; but its occupants did enjoy some comforts and luxuries, as evidenced by the substantial sherds from Mediterranean amphorae once containing expensive olive oil and red wine.

From the supposed site of Arthur's birth at Tintagel it is a short distance to that of his fatal wounding in combat by Mordred at **Slaughterbridge**. An inscribed stone lies here, picturesquely covered with moss, in apparent neglect by the banks of the river. It is now no longer considered to be connected to the death of Arthur but to that of a later Celtic chieftain; yet in popular mythology this is Arthur's grave, and always will be. Such is the power of the Arthurian magic, that once even a flimsy association has been established, it is impossible for it ever to be expunged from the record. There are hundreds of Arthurian sites scattered the length of Britain, but the most serious contenders are those of Cornwall and Somerset; and it is straight to Somerset that this journey now leads.

South Cadbury in the south of the county is a peaceful village lying in the shadow of the powerful Iron Age hillfort of **Cadbury Castle** which was refortified in the closing decades of the fifth century and equipped with a timber hall commensurate with the status of a regional chieftain or king. As with Tintagel, the evidence at Cadbury Castle is a far cry from the later vision of Camelot as a lofty, battlemented castle of stone. Interestingly, those same sherds of

Mediterranean pottery as discovered at Tintagel, showed up again in the course of the excavations at Cadbury. If we accept that this was Arthur in both places, then the 'once and future king' was consistently loyal to his suppliers of wine and oil.

The last leg of this quest for the elusive Arthur takes us to **Glastonbury**, where the legend of the Dark Ages eventually resurfaced in the Middle Ages, when the monks of **Glastonbury Abbey** claimed to have located the actual grave of Arthur and Guinevere. Needless to say, the matter can no longer be put to the test, since the skeletons have disappeared along with the lead cross identifying Arthur. No matter, the abbey quickly grew rich on the proceeds of the Arthurian pilgrimages and was able to rebuild in magnificent style. A hotel was opened in the town to lodge the wealthier visitors, and it is still in business as the George and Pilgrim. Unfortunately, the great riches of the abbey were indirectly responsible in bringing about the gruesome execution of the last Abbot of Glastonbury at the time of the Dissolution. This aged monk sought to conceal some of Glastonbury Abbey's expensive plate from the Commissioners of Henry VIII. As punishment for this attempted purloining of the King's property, the elderly abbot was dragged to the top of Glastonbury Tor and put to death. His body was quartered and sent to Wells, Bath, Ilchester and Bridgwater as a grim reminder to others. The head was spiked on the gate of Glastonbury Abbey.

The summit of **Glastonbury Tor** is occupied by the isolated tower of St Michael, all that remains of a church on the spot. It enjoys a vast panorama across the wide expanse of the Somerset Levels, once the refuge of Alfred the Great. Some say the hill is hollow and that King Arthur and his Knights of the Round Table are sleeping inside it, but will awake and ride forth on Judgement Day. This is a powerful and magical place where history and myth, brutal reality and poetic legend come together in a unique potion that is quintessentially medieval. Those who debunk the Arthurian legend would do well to remember that factual inconsistencies posed no problems to the people of the Middle Ages who believed in such stories. Indeed, they were spiritual meat and drink to both rich and poor. It is worth pausing on the summit of Glastonbury Tor, where so many strands of that rich medieval tapestry are interwoven, to reflect on both the faith and the credulity of medieval England, before descending the hill and stepping back into the twentieth century once more.

Interrupted conversation at Crowland Abbey in Lincolnshire.

EPILOGUE

THE JOURNEYS DESCRIBED and illustrated in this book should be seen as doors or windows giving partial access to a world that has receded in time though not disappeared completely from view. Additional volumes could easily be filled with places and relics from the Middle Ages which – for reasons of space – could not all be accommodated between these covers. The overriding aim of this account has been to convey a vivid impression of the amazing depth and diversity of England's medieval heritage. The need to be selective has meant making some difficult omissions; and the reader's attention is drawn to the books mentioned in the bibliography, some of which contain more comprehensive listings.

Parish churches and cathedrals are undoubtedly the strongest living links we possess to the medieval past where an unbroken chain of humans at prayer binds us to the remote but familiar world of distant ancestors. However, the headstones in the graveyards are usually no older than Georgian, so we are by and large confronted with the anonymous ghosts of the Middle Ages rather than by individuals with documented histories. The exceptions are the great men and women of the feudal magnate class whose proud effigies still repose in canopied niches and chantry chapels, often dominating the modest interior of the parish church. Great works of art they are for sure, and many exquisite pieces of sculpture; but they have a social message as well. Did they not remind the rank-and-file of the population, even during the religious services, of their subordinate standing in this world and of their obligations to their temporal masters and mistresses?

It is interesting to reflect that the descendants of the powerful landowning families, though still in many cases in possession of large estates, are now confronted by a rather different world. While their ancestors ruled the roost and ordinary folk were beholden to them in most aspects of their lives, today we encounter them as the hereditary custodians of the ancestral pile, well versed in public relations and tourism marketing, anxious to attract local people and foreign visitors in order to defray the immense costs of maintaining a historic house. Some families gave up the struggle and passed the baton to the National Trust, which now owns a number of ancient properties of outstanding importance. The price of membership can easily be recouped just by visiting National Trust houses of medieval origin.

The intricate Percy tomb canopy in Beverley Minster.

Certainly the largest proprietor of medieval real estate in the land – albeit on behalf of the nation – is English Heritage. Their collection consists principally of abandoned buildings that became too dilapidated to be converted or were too impractical to accommodate the changing requirements of domestic comfort. While some people prefer a lived-in house with an accretion of the styles and devices of various ages, others feel more freedom and a more tangible sense of times past in a naked ruin. For the connoisseur a good ruin should have enough left to give an overall idea of how the building once looked. Items of decorative detail have a poignancy of their own. A carving on a column or a slender lancet window in a broken wall can touch the emotions quite unexpectedly.

English Heritage has done much in recent years to bring the medieval past to life with its restoration work, interpretive displays, special events and publications. But sometimes you find yourself wishing they wouldn't mow the grass quite so often and would allow some ivy a tenuous toe-hold in the ancient masonry to add a dimension of natural magic much appreciated by those with a taste for romantic relics. Nevertheless, no one with an interest in medieval England should be without English Heritage membership, for it holds the key to scores of beautiful monuments all over the country.

Fascination with the past need be neither obsessive nor retrogressive. Indeed, it is often those with their feet well planted in the era of modern technology, such as architects and engineers, who can respond most positively to the physical achievements of the Middle Ages. As time-travellers we should feel free to come and go as we please. But for all our efforts we can only grope in the dark as we try to imagine the reality of a world without aeroplanes, trains, cars, motorways, telephones, fax machines and television – a society that functioned with none of the apparatus of the electronic age. Somehow, all that has to be temporarily banished from the mind if we are to feel and comprehend the reality of medieval England as it was lived and experienced at the time.

Bibliography

Alexander, Jonathan & Binski, Paul (ed.), *Age of Chivalry: Art in Plantagenet England*, Royal Academy of Arts/Weidenfeld & Nicolson 1987
Betjeman, John (ed.), *Collins Guide to Parish Churches of England & Wales*, Collins 1980
Braun, Hugh *An Introduction to English Medieval Architecture*, Faber & Faber 1968
— *Cathedral Architecture*, Faber & Faber 1972
— *English Abbeys*, Faber & Faber 1971
— *Parish Churches*, Faber & Faber 1974
Clifton-Taylor, Alec, *The Cathedrals of England*, Thames & Hudson 1986
Johnson, Paul, *National Trust Book of British Castles*, Weidenfeld & Nicolson 1978
Kerr, Nigel & Mary, *A Guide to Medieval Sites in Britain*, Grafton Books 1988
King, Edmund, *Medieval England*, Phaidon 1988
Loyn, H.R. (ed.), *The Middle Ages – A Concise Encyclopedia*, Thames & Hudson 1989
Morris, Richard, *Cathedrals and Abbeys of England & Wales*, J.M. Dent 1979
Muir, Richard, *National Trust Guide to the Dark Ages and Medieval Britain*, George Philip 1985
New, Anthony, *A Guide to the Abbeys of England and Wales*, Constable 1985
Platt, Colin, *The Castle in Medieval England and Wales*, Secker & Warburg 1982
— *The Abbeys and Priories of Medieval England*, Secker & Warburg 1984
— *National Trust Guide to Late Medieval and Renaissance Britain*, George Philip 1986
Rowley, Trevor, *The High Middle Ages*, Routledge & Kegan Paul 1986
— *The Norman Heritage*, Routledge & Kegan Paul 1983
Saul, Nigel, *Batsford Companion to Medieval England*, Batsford 1983
Smith, Edwin, *English Parish Churches*, Thames & Hudson 1976

INDEX

Numbers in italics refer to illustrations